BLACK WINGS

VON HARDESTY

BLACK WINGS

Courageous Stories of African Americans in Aviation and Space History

Collins
An Imprint of HarperCollinsPublishers

IN ASSOCIATION WITH THE
SMITHSONIAN NATIONAL AIR AND SPACE MUSEUM

HarperCollins books may be purchased for educational, business, or sales promotional use. For information, please write: Special Markets Department, HarperCollins Publishers, 10 East 53rd Street, New York, NY 10022.

FIRST EDITION

Designed by Lovedog Studio

Printed on acid-free paper
Library of Congress Cataloging-in-Publication Data
Hardesty, Von, 1939-
Black wings : courageous stories of African Americans in aviation and space history / Von Hardesty. —1st ed.
p. cm.
"In association with the Smithsonian National Air and Space Museum."
Includes bibliographical references and index.
ISBN 978-0-06-126138-1
1. African American air pilots—Biography. 2. African American astronauts—Biography. 3. Air pilots—United States—Biography. 4. Astronauts—United States—Biography. I. Title.
TL539.H285 2007
629.13092 '296073—dc22
[B]

2007021270

07 08 09 10 11 TOP 10 9 8 7 6 5 4 3 2 1

Dedicated to the memory of
Theodore W. Robinson, 1926–2001

CONTENTS

FOREWORD

Very early in my life I decided that I would fly airplanes. This love for flying was not based on any firsthand experience, but acquired, I'm certain, because my dad would take me to military air shows and exposed me to the beauty and grandeur of those powerful machines as they rolled and looped and climbed into the heavens. In those days, outings such as these were considered essential for the development and preparation of the young. The segregated school system in Washington, DC, where I grew up during the late 1940s and 1950s, provided young Negroes the opportunity to experience and be taught by excellent and extremely motivated and passionate scholars. As I reflect on this time, I feel privileged to have experienced and benefited from the comprehensive education offered and the preparation it provided for my future endeavors. A theme repeated often, not just in school, but also in the neighborhood, the church, and at home was that we as a people were at least equal, that we were significant, and that we would contribute.

Our knowledge of African Americans who had made major contributions was extremely limited. There was, of course, nothing written in our school books, nor were there any other sources that we could easily reference describing the discoveries, inventions, political influence and impact, risks and the heroism of those men and women of color who would have been our role models. Years would pass before any acknowledgment of these contributions and the significance of each would be written.

Von Hardesty's *Black Wings: Courageous Stories of African Americans in Aviation and Space History* is such a defining document. Though this is a book about people in isolation and their accomplishments and sacrifices, it is written in a way that shows the natural linkage and dependence each had on the generation before. The impact that the Wright brothers had, Von Hardesty points out, was not limited to a specific racial group. There were young African Americans who also read with pride the press reports of flight on the sand dunes of North Carolina and were also excited about the possibility of solo flight. Unfortunately that opportunity was only offered beyond the continental boundaries of the United States.

Bessie Coleman and Eugene Bullard never imagined that traveling to France in the early 1900s to win their right and privilege to fly would have a profound influence on aviation in America. All they wanted to do was fly. Their passion to participate overwhelmingly dictated their direction even though they had been told that Negroes weren't smart enough to do such things.

The Tuskegee Airmen demonstrated repeatedly during World War II that they were at least equal and very significant as they protected the bomber crews and aircraft flying dangerous missions into the war zones of Europe. These airmen, Davis, Hall, Roberts, Driver, Gleed, Lester, and scores of others believed that by performing heroic tasks and doing important things that they would achieve long sought equality. Though equality wasn't immediate, many were watching and the path soon led to the integrated military force. Civilian integration lagged behind but soon America realized that its strength and capability could only be achieved by inclusion, not exclusion.

Aviation has become a part of all of our lives. What began as an exception or oddity evolved into the expected and norm. I was influenced to compete to be an astronaut by Lieutenant General Benjamin O. Davis Jr., commander of the first Negro fighter squadron. I had known him since I was very young. As I debated whether I should spend the time completing the application, General Davis called, encouraging me to apply not just because he asked but also in honor of the Tuskegee Airmen. In 1977, I did not know who the Tuskegee Airmen were. When he told me who they were and what they had accomplished, I felt great pride and realized that my ability to choose was forged by the airmen and by those who smoothed the path before and after them.

Aviation history gathered in this outstanding book by Von Hardesty captures and compiles that missing history. It is clear after reading his book that we were at least equal, that we were significant, and that we did contribute.

Frederick D. Gregory, USAF Colonel (Ret.)
Astronaut and former NASA Deputy Administrator

INTRODUCTION

Colin Powell once observed that "a dream doesn't become reality through magic; it takes sweat, determination, and hard work." This axiom is mirrored dramatically in the story of African Americans in aerospace history. The invention of the airplane in the first decade of the twentieth century sparked a revolution in modern technology. This new realm of powered flight rapidly altered modes of travel and recast the conduct of warfare. Aviation in the popular mind became associated with adventure and heroism. For African Americans, however, this exciting new realm of flying remained off-limits, a consequence of racial discrimination. Many African Americans displayed a keen interest in the new air age, but found themselves routinely barred from getting training as pilots or mechanics. This pattern of racial bias became enshrined in the elite Army Air Corps, where blacks were denied admission on racial grounds. Beginning in the 1920s, a small and widely scattered group of black air enthusiasts challenged this prevailing pattern of racial discrimination. With no small amount of effort—and against formidable odds—they gained their pilot licenses and acquired the technical skills to become aircraft mechanics. Their dream became a concrete reality through Powell's formula of "sweat, determination, and hard work."

Black Wings: Courageous Stories of African Americans in Aviation and Space History offers the reader an overview of this extraordinary saga. Black aerospace pioneers—as pilots, astronauts, technicians, scientists, and administrators—have made important strides toward racial tolerance. Their story is not an isolated one, but a pivotal chapter in the ongoing quest for racial equality in the American experience.

As a new book, *Black Wings: Courageous Stories of African Americans in Aviation and Space History* reflects a long tradition of research and exhibit work at the National Air and Space Museum (NASM). In 1982, the museum opened its landmark exhibit: "Black Wings: The American Black in Aviation." An exhibit catalog of the same name followed a year later. These two events represented a concerted effort at the Smithsonian Institution to chronicle a lost dimension of American history. The Black Wings exhibit quickly attracted a huge following, serving as a catalyst for myriad new books, film documentaries, and research projects. The exhibit catalog, *Black Wings: The American Black in Aviation*, enjoyed remarkable popularity over the course of a quarter century, boasting eight separate printings. All these museum-based activities have dovetailed with a larger trend of new research and histories dealing with story of black aerospace pioneers.

The creation of the original Black Wings Exhibit benefited greatly from the creative work of a large number of people. The late Theodore Robinson, who as an independent historian gathered key data on the early black aviators, made a substantial and sustained contribution. He freely donated his time and expertise to the National Air and Space Museum; this book is dedicated to his memory. Donald S. Lopez, currently deputy director of NASM, paved the way for the original exhibit to become a reality. He assigned Von Hardesty and Dominick Pisano, both curators in the Museum's Aeronautics Division, to be responsible for the creation of the Black Wings exhibit and catalog. As curators, Hardesty and Pisano have overseen many programs related to the Black Wings historical theme, including research, publications, and public inquiries. Other NASM staff worked actively in this subject area, most notably planning for a new and expanded Black Wings exhibition: "Dream to Fly." Exhibit designer Linda King has been active in this arena of future planning, along with Cathleen Lewis of the Space History Division, assisted by Ian Cook, who gathered a substantial amount of historical materials, oral histories, and photographs in the 1990s. Alison Mitchell, working with Clare Cuddy of the Museum's Education Department, Theodore Robinson, and Von Hardesty fashioned a dedicated museum website to the story of Black Wings; this site was designed to assist teachers and researchers. These varied programs represent the creative backdrop for the publication of *Black Wings: Courageous Stories of African Americans in Aviation and Space History*.

The National Air and Space Museum has also benefited from the research of outside experts. Philip S. Hart, who developed the PBS documentary *Flyers in Search of a Dream* (1987), found and restored one of the last remaining copies of William J. Powell's 1935 film *Unemployment, the Negro, and Aviation*. The late Benjamin O. Davis Jr. and his late wife, Agatha Davis, assisted with the original exhibit and served as advisers to the museum on many activities associated with the Black Wings exhibit. Marjorie Kriz and Jill Snider, researchers on early black aviation pioneers, provided new details and insights on what had been perceived as a lost history. Finally, there were a large group of African American aviation veterans, some now deceased, who made their individual contributions, beginning with the museum's own Lou Purnell and including Chauncey Spencer, Janet Bragg, Cornelius Coffey, Howard Hurd, William Thompson, Neil Loving, Elmer Jones, Clarence D. Lester, A. A. Rayner Jr., and William Brown, among many others.

There are a number of individuals associated with the National Air and Space Museum who deserve special mention for their work on *Black Wings: Courageous Stories of African Americans in Aviation and Space History*. Patricia J. Graboske, publications head at the museum, played a key role in overseeing and managing the new book project. Larry DiRicco made it his quest to locate new photographs and illustrations. Mike Moore conducted baseline research on the Tuskegee airmen. Dom Pisano and Cathleen Lewis offered advice about preparing the narrative for this book. Many others played valuable roles in bringing the book to press: Ted Hamady, Barbara Brennan, Eric Long, Paula Green, Flint Whitlock, Betty Gubert, Elizabeth Laney, Kristine Kaske-Martin, and Kate Igoe. The HarperCollins staff also deserve special mention: Donna Sanzone, executive editor; Stephanie Meyers, assistant editor; Georgia Morrisey, cover design; Shubhani Sarkar, interior design; and the production staff, including Diane Aronson, Vivian Gomez, and Karen Lumley.

Bessie Coleman stands next to her JN-4 Curtiss Jenny biplane.

CHAPTER 1

BARNSTORMER BESSIE COLEMAN TAKES TO THE AIR

THE AIR AGE BEGAN WHEN THE WRIGHT BROTHERS made their successful flight at Kitty Hawk on December 17, 1903. That first aerial trek consisted of a mere 120 feet. It was a modest leap into the air, but it signaled a revolution. Today, the airplane is a powerful and lethal weapon of war. Moreover, airliners routinely transport millions of passengers around the globe. The airplane became identified with adventure and progress. The birth of aviation in the United States, however, coincided with the era of Jim Crow, a climate of formal and informal racial discrimination. African Americans—as a group—found themselves excluded from most spheres of modern technology and from this new exciting realm of aviation. One young woman from Chicago broke this barrier of racial prejudice: Bessie Coleman.

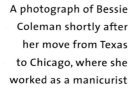

A photograph of Bessie Coleman shortly after her move from Texas to Chicago, where she worked as a manicurist

When Bessie Coleman traveled to France in November 1920, her first trip abroad, she was determined to gain a coveted prize: a pilot's license from the Fédération Aéronautique Internationale (FAI). Earning the FAI license brought special distinction, but even more so for a woman. Coleman had traveled from Chicago to a distant aerodrome in Le Crotoy in northern France to inaugurate her unusual flying career.

For Coleman, the quest to become a licensed pilot reflected a deep and abiding passion. As a young African American woman, she endured enormous racial prejudice at home. The prevailing Jim

One of the first African Americans to fly was Eugene Bullard. A native of Georgia, Bullard emigrated to France, where he joined the French infantry in World War I. He then flew briefly with the French in 1917, the same year the United States entered the war.

Crow practices in the United States had effectively denied her access to aeronautical training—as it had for all aspiring black aviators at the time. She worked tirelessly to raise money for the trip and eventually enrolled in the École d'Aviation des Frères Caudron (the Caudron Brothers' Aviation School). The flight training curriculum at the Caudron Brothers' school was strict and unforgiving, especially for a female cadet who had so much to prove. The FAI license was hers if she could complete the rigorous course of study. Coleman understood this license was a ticket for her to pursue an aviation career in the United States.

The flight school was located near Le Crotoy in the Somme region of northern France. In fact, Bessie's flight training at the Caudron meant she would be flying in the same skies where many great air battles had raged during the Great War (1914–1918). Her flight training consisted of mastering the essential skills to control and maneuver an airplane. The Caudron school used the durable French Nieuport Type 82 trainer, a two-place, open-cockpit biplane. Built of wood and fabric, the Nieuport biplane was highly nimble and forgiving, and therefore ideal for teaching the essential flying maneuvers. Bessie later described these maneuvers as "tail spins, banking and looping the loop."

Coleman earned her FAI license on June 15, 1921. For the young American, this moment represented an important milestone. She took great pride in her achievement, as it had been a long and difficult road from rural Texas to Chicago to France for pilot training. Her passion for flying had overcome numerous challenges and barriers, culminating in a real individual triumph against considerable odds. On a larger level, the FAI license established an important precedent, one that would cast a long shadow for all African Americans seeking to enter aviation in the decades ahead—Bessie Coleman was the first African American woman to gain the coveted FAI license.

Born in Atlanta in 1892, Bessie Coleman grew up in Waxahachie, Texas, a small town located some 30 miles south of Dallas. Her family existed in the poverty of the cotton fields of Texas. Survival in this harsh economic reality depended on hard work with the minimal rewards that came with the sharecropping system. Her father—who was part Native American by heritage—left the family when Bessie was nine years old. One of thirteen children, she spent a considerable amount of time working and caring for her younger siblings. Although she and her family lived in poverty, she took great pleasure in learning. Bessie excelled in school and, in 1910, entered a preparatory school at the Agricultural and Normal College in Langston, Oklahoma. Bessie's sojourn at the college, however, proved short-lived, largely because she lacked funding for tuition and living expenses. Returning to Texas, she resumed the difficult life of a domestic worker, often earning money as a laundress. Finally, in 1915, she left Waxahachie for Chicago to seek her fortune. She stayed with her brother, Walter, and enrolled in beauty school. To make ends meet, she worked tirelessly as cook, maid, and manicurist.

Federation Aéronautique
Internationale
FRANCE

Nous soussignés pouvoir sportif
reconnu par la Fédération
Aéronautique Internationale
pour la France certifions que:

Mme Bessie Coleman
né a Atlanta, Texas
le 20 Janvier 1896
ayant rempli toutes les conditions
imposées par la F.A.I. a été breveté

Pilote-Aviateur
a la date du 15 Juin 1921
Commission Sportive Aéronautique
le Président:

Signature du Titulaire
Bessie Coleman

N° du Brevet 18.310.

Bessie Coleman received her pilot's license from the Fédération Aéronautique Internationale on June 15, 1921.

How and why Coleman became interested in flying remains uncertain, but the spark may have come from reading newspaper accounts of aviators and learning of the exploits of a small band of women flyers. Robert S. Abbott, the publisher of the *Chicago Defender*, befriended her and suggested she learn French and enroll in a flying school in France. Bessie saved her money and subordinated her entire life to the quest to learn to fly. In 1921, after seven months of rigorous training, she obtained the FAI license and in 1922, she returned to France to complete an advanced course of flight training.

In time, Coleman began to break out of the shadows and attract the notice of the black press. Being a legitimate aviatrix, she began to forge her plans for a career in aviation. Since she still lacked the personal finances required to support full-time work in flying, she sought out patrons and supporters. Despite the racial discrimination of the time, she persevered and worked effectively to dramatize her skills as a licensed pilot. Her debut as a stunt pilot came in September 1922, when she appeared at Curtiss Field outside New York City, an event to honor the veterans of the all-black 369th Infantry Regiment that had participated in the American Expeditionary Force in World War I. Her patron, Robert Abbott, played a key role in arranging the air show, proclaiming Coleman as "the world's greatest woman flyer."

After enjoying this pivotal triumph, she returned to her hometown of Chicago for an air show at Checkerboard Airdrome (present-day Midway Airport). In Chicago, Coleman enlisted the support of another patron, David L. Behncke, the president of the International Airline Pilots Association.

Fueled by her success, Bessie Coleman aspired to be part of the world of barnstorming, which swept over aviation in the 1920s and attracted huge crowds. The barnstormers were a special breed: addicted to adventure and ready to push their fragile aircraft to the limit with dangerous aerobatic maneuvers. The term *barnstorming* originated in the theater; it referred to a troupe of itinerant actors who, in the absence of a theater or opera house in the provinces, performed in barns. The term was a good fit for the touring stunt pilots who performed death-defying aerobatics or offered plane rides to locals in the 1920s. Because few towns and cities had airports in those days, barnstormers often set up their air shows in open fields. Even Charles Lindbergh—the air hero of the age after his 1927 transatlantic flight—tried his hand at barnstorming as a youth. Lindbergh purchased a war surplus Jenny biplane to earn money as a barnstormer, touring the Western states for a season. Bessie Coleman also flew the Jenny, which was one of the more popular aircraft used by stunt pilots. The fabled Jenny was a slow and highly maneuverable airplane—and, for the inexperienced pilot, a forgiving flying machine. Still, a Jenny could be dangerous; the primitive aircraft of that era were vulnerable to sudden engine shutdowns and structural failure if stressed too hard in wild aerobatic maneuvers.

For Bessie, barnstorming offered a siren call—a compelling way to earn money, acquire celebrity, and make her way in the male-dominated world of aviation. Her training in France had prepared her well for the rigors and dangers of this pastime—flying figure eights, tailspins, loops, and barrel rolls. Most women who participated in the barnstormer circuit were wing walkers, not pilots. Bessie offered a contrast to the typical routine: the rarity of witnessing a woman—in this case a black woman—at the controls of an airplane. Bessie found it intoxicating to compete with other intrepid aviators in such air shows, and took delight in the fact that her aerial stunts popularized aviation in the black community.

The barnstorming world was characterized by intense competition. It offered limited financial rewards to a select few who mustered an optimal blend of talent and luck. Some barnstormers worked alone, eking out an uncertain income on extended sum-

Bessie Coleman dressed in her flying outfit with its military look—high-top boots, Sam Browne belt, jodhpurs, leather jacket, helmet, and goggles.

As a pioneering barnstormer, Coleman allied herself with a number of patrons, sponsors, and managers.

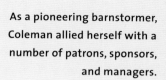

The Elite Circle and Girl's DeLuxe Club sponsor an Aerial Frolic with a jazz band to honor Bessie Coleman as Chicago's pioneering aviatrix. Date unknown.

mer tours across the country. However, there were some well-financed and profitable organizations that exploited the financial windfalls directly associated with barnstorming by visiting larger urban centers where they could draw paying onlookers. These groups became known as *flying circuses*. There was the Gates Flying Circus, which owned a fleet of aircraft and employed a large crew of barnstorming pilots, one of whom was the daring performer Clyde "Upside Down" Pangborn. With such a large troupe of fliers and performers, the Gates organization drew large crowds to watch loops and spins, high-speed flybys, parachuting, formation flights, and spine-tingling stunts in which a person would transfer from one plane to another in the air.

Bessie Coleman thrived in this exciting world of aerial stunts and daredevil flying. She fully understood that the public persona of the successful barnstormer required no small measure of flamboyance and self-promotion. Bessie learned to dress the part—wearing jodhpurs and quasi-military garb, a silk scarf, a flying helmet, and goggles. To be a barnstomer required great showmanship; therefore, Bessie soon embraced all the exaggeration and posturing that went with the profession, telling truths, half-truths, and even untruths about her flying career. For those who promoted Bessie Coleman, the barnstormer lifestyle became essential—and it was a key element in assuring their financial success.

Bessie did find her way into the realm of barnstorming, but her career was a turbulent one. As a barnstormer, she demonstrated the typical boldness and opportunism that came with the air show circuits. In the final analysis, one did not survive long without also demonstrating skill as a pilot. Coleman received the plaudits of

Visit the Flying Circus Today

A Ride For Everybody

Experience the thrills of the air in one of our large planes

Clyde E. Pangborn, first man to fly upside down, and chief pilot of Gates Flying Circus, with his plane in inverted position in inset.

TODAY AND MONDAY   MARCH 4-5

See Gainesville from high in the skies--- The thrill of your lifetime and at a very moderate cost too. . . .

Stunt Flying and FREE tickets will be features today at noon. Watch for the planes and the copies of the Gainesville Sun which will be dropped during the stunt flying act.

Special arrangements for parties wishing to fly together.

GATES FLYING CIRCUS

JARVIS FIELD   THE BIG TEXACO PLANES

Barnstormers in the 1920s were often organized into touring groups, such as the Gates Flying Circus.

BESS

Spirit ... Coleman ... revealed by Rev. J. C. Austin, in organizing ... group of aviators, Sunday May 2...

The Chicago-based Challenger Air Pilots' Association sponsored a flying event each year to honor Bessie Coleman.

other barnstormers for her bravery and competence as an aviator. There were few licensed black pilots in the barnstorming world; a notable exception was the flamboyant and controversial Hubert Julian. Unlike Coleman, Julian left a trail of broken promises and was charged with being a huckster. Julian often failed to show up for performances, crashed airplanes of would-be patrons, and launched grandiose schemes, never fulfilled, to fly across the continent or the Atlantic Ocean—schemes that never came to reality. If Julian was an embarrassment to the small community of black air enthusiasts, Coleman became an inspirational figure.

Bessie's barnstorming career gained considerable attention in the black press as she continued to perform across the country. It was always a challenge to raise sufficient funds to purchase aircraft and sustain her life on the air show circuit. She often combined lecturing with air shows to keep her career in motion. At one point, she agreed to participate in a movie titled *Shadow and Sunshine*, but then abruptly withdrew, a decision that won her animosity and sparked a deluge of negative publicity. One of Coleman's reasons for abandoning the movie project was the requirement that she appear as poor woman, dressed in rags and walking with a cane—she had decided that she would not play out existing racial stereotypes. This incident mirrored dramatically Coleman's fidelity to her own sense of propriety. She had consistently advocated progress for her race, working to establish a flying school for black youth. For Bessie Coleman, the showmanship of stunt flying did not mean that she would repudiate her core commitment to end racial discrimination.

Frequent reversals punctuated Coleman's life on the air show circuit. In 1923, she managed to purchase an inexpensive Curtiss Jenny in California. The aircraft was old and not all that reliable, but affordable. Bessie flew the old Jenny from Santa Monica to Los Angeles, but it proved to be a difficult aircraft to handle. Bessie found herself unable to prevent a stall, which led to a nosedive. In the resulting crash, she broke a leg and several ribs, and was hospitalized for three months and spent eighteen months recuperating in Chicago with her family. She resumed her flying career in Texas, which proved to be a huge success.

As an African American, Coleman wanted to break the general silence in the mainstream media. The black press had been sympathetic and offered regular coverage of her aerial exploits, seeing these as a new benchmark for her race. The white-owned newspapers, however, were less predictable in their coverage. Bessie strived energetically to garner attention from the mainstream media outlets and attract local political figures to her air shows. In August 1923, Governor Vic Donahey of Ohio sent Bessie a letter expressing a "hearty welcome" to the Labor Day celebration in Columbus. The mayor of Columbus, in an apparently coordinated gesture, also wrote to her, expressing the same warm welcome and expressing the hope that her "stay in our city will be pleasant and profitable." The mayor made reference to Coleman's career, which he described as one of "skill, daring, and courage."

Throughout her flying career in the 1920s, Bessie increasingly turned to lectures to generate enthusiasm for aviation and raise the funds she needed to help support her work. She also recruited, and alienated, a number of managers and agents. Those who abandoned Coleman often complained of her temperamental and demanding personality. In the span of her career, she had five different managers in just twenty-eight months. She spent the last year of her life on a whirlwind lecture tour showing film clips of her aerial stunts in a move to get public support. These efforts proved ineffectual and her financial situation only worsened. Now desperate for funding, she moved to Orlando, Florida, and opened a beauty shop.

Bessie Coleman died in Florida in 1926. The events leading up to her tragic end remain clouded with some mystery and controversy. In the hope of getting back into flying, Coleman turned to Edwin M. Beeman, the son of the chewing gum mogul Harry L. Beeman, for financial support. The younger Beeman assisted her in the purchase of a used Army JN-4 biplane, which was flown from Dallas to Jacksonville by a young white mechanic named William D. Wells. The plane's condition was marginal at best, and Wells had been forced to make more than one emergency landing on the long trek from Texas. Wells landed the JN-4 at Paxon Field in Jacksonville on April 28, 1926. Observers at the airfield later reported that the airplane's engine, a 90 horsepower OX-5, was tired and unreliable.

Coleman planned to fly her airplane on May Day in an air show sponsored by the Negro Welfare League of Jacksonville. On the day before the event, she joined Wells on test flight. She asked the mechanic to take the front seat and guide the plane around the airfield so she could study the geography of the airstrip. Since she was small of stature, she unfastened her seat belt to allow her to see over the side of the airplane. Wells flew the JN-4 to 2,000 feet and circled for five minutes; then, he pushed the airplane up to 3,500 feet and banked back toward Paxon Field. Some observers noted that the JN-4 abruptly gained speed and then nosedived to the ground, falling into a spin at around 1,000 feet. Once the aircraft started its uncontrolled descent, it suddenly flipped over—probably at an altitude of merely 500 feet. Bessie—who was flying without a seat belt or parachute—fell to the ground in a series of somersaults. She was killed instantly upon hitting the ground; nearly every bone in her body was broken. Wells crashed with the plane and also died. It was later discovered that an errant wrench had jammed the controls on the JN-4.

Doris Rich, author of *Queen Bess*, the definitive biography of Bessie Coleman, has pointed to certain factors that have fueled her powerful legacy: "zeal for life . . . [and] that ephemeral daydream of adventure, strength, audacity and beauty . . ." It appears that her death only enlarged her image as a pioneer female pilot. By the end of the 1920s, a new generation of black aviators emerged, and these fliers—men and women—found inspiration in the life of Bessie Coleman. Los Angeles inaugurated the Bessie Coleman Flying Club and black pilots in Chicago sponsored an annual flyby in her honor.

In 1927, the silent film, *The Flying Ace*, made its debut, promising "thrills" and "action." The all-black cast dealt with the popular theme of aviation at a time when racial discrimination excluded African Americans from flying.

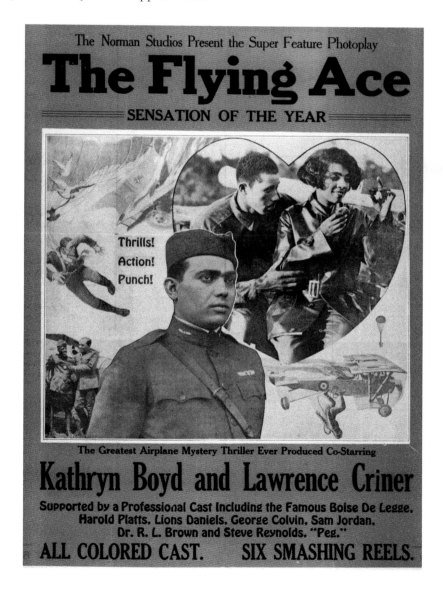

The Norman Studios Present the Super Feature Photoplay

The Flying Ace

SENSATION OF THE YEAR

Thrills!
Action!
Punch!

The Greatest Airplane Mystery Thriller Ever Produced Co-Starring

Kathryn Boyd and Lawrence Criner

Supported by a Professional Cast Including the Famous Boise De Legge, Harold Platts, Lions Daniels, George Colvin, Sam Jordan, Dr. R. L. Brown and Steve Reynolds, "Peg."

ALL COLORED CAST.   **SIX SMASHING REELS.**

William J. Powell Jr. was a visionary and high-energy promoter of aviation in the African American community in the 1930s. He wrote the classic book *Black Wings* (1934) to encourage black youth to become pilots and aviation mechanics. He believed that aviation was a new and pioneering realm of modern technology with vast opportunities for black youth.

CHAPTER 2

FACING THE HEADWINDS OF PREJUDICE

THE GOLDEN AGE OF FLIGHT IS REMEMBERED FOR ITS air shows, record-breaking flights, and air heroes. This extraordinary period in aviation history extended throughout two decades, roughly from 1920 to 1940. One flight stands out above the many stellar aerial feats in this age of heroism: Charles Lindbergh's solo transatlantic flight in May 1927. He became an instant global celebrity, as did many other male and female fliers, who established new records in the quest to fly faster, higher, and further. For example, American pilots Amelia Earhart, Wiley Post, and Jimmy Doolittle made headlines with their flying exploits. The airplane moved to the forefront of American life, offering a new mode of transportation to trains and automobiles. Soon pioneer airlines took shape and began to offer travelers a new—and often speedy—way to travel between cities, even from one coast to the other. In the military sphere, in both the army and the navy, aviation was no longer a novelty, but a vital branch of the armed forces, thought by some theorists to be the decisive weapon in any future war. Simply put, the airplane occupied a special place at the epicenter of national life, the object of popular fascination as the most advanced sphere of modern technology.

African Americans were drawn to this new world of aviation, as were all Americans, sharing the widespread interest in aeronautical progress. However, blacks who aspired to become pilots were routinely barred from participation in the new aeronautical world. Typically, they could not gain entrance to aviation schools to learn to fly nor could they even qualify as aircraft mechanics. The Army

Cover of *Craftsmen of Aero-News*, June 1937, with William J. Powell Jr. and women air enthusiasts in Los Angeles.

Air Corps, then the most elite branch of military aviation, denied blacks access to flight training, arguing that they lacked the necessary aptitude to fly modern aircraft. Racial exclusion cast a shadow over the fast-growing aviation sector. Few blacks managed to obtain pilot licenses, but only after extreme effort: for example, C. Alfred Anderson, a Philadelphia youth who yearned to fly, had to first purchase his own plane and then hire a flight instructor to teach him the basics. As new municipal airports opened, there were few job possibilities for blacks, aside from performing unskilled labor or working as skycaps. By the 1930s, it appeared that aviation—in the same fashion as the railroads—would be segregated.

African Americans effectively surmounted these racial barriers by establishing flying clubs in Los Angeles and Chicago. During the difficult years of the Great Depression, few people had the financial resources to buy their own airplanes or pay for flight lessons; therefore, they pooled together their limited resources, so they could purchase or rent airplanes or seek out flight instructors for training. By gathering a small cadre of trained pilots and mechanics, blacks were able to expand their opportunities for flying dramatically. Many of the early black pioneers were keenly appealing to the black community for support. The recruitment of youth, in particular, became a high priority.

LOS ANGELES: REMEMBERING BESSIE COLEMAN

A small group of black aviation enthusiasts appeared in Los Angeles as early as 1929. One figure stood out, a man named William J. Powell Jr., who emerged as the driving force behind the campaign to organize the first black flying club in the city. He had moved from Chicago to Southern California in 1928 to attend the Warren School of Aeronautics and had earned his pilot's license upon graduation. He realized that a flying club would be the most effective way to realize his personal dream of rallying the black community to join the new aeronautical world. Accordingly, he launched the Bessie Coleman Aero Club in 1931, which quickly became the venue for a series of early milestones in the 1930s—air shows, evening classes for flight training, long-distance flying records, and a variety of promotional efforts that included a book titled *Black Wings*, a documentary film, a stage play, and a trade journal.

William J. Powell Jr. offered aviation scholarships through his Craftsmen of Black Wings organization.

Powell's decision to seek out flight training represented an important turning point in his life. He previously had followed a more terrestrial career path as a successful businessman on Chicago's south side. Born in Henderson, Kentucky, in 1899, William's original surname had been Jennifer, although little is known about his biological father. When William was four years old, his father died. By 1904, his widowed mother decided to escape the rural poverty of Kentucky, taking William and his younger sister, Edna, to the bustling metropolis of Chicago—then a magnet for many African Americans from the South seeking a better life. William's mother eventually remarried a man from Arkansas named Powell, and the children then adopted Powell as their new surname.

Powell had attended Wendell Phillips High School where he excelled in his academic studies. Gifted musically, he also played the piano and sang in the choir of Ebenezer Baptist Church. Upon graduating from high school, Powell entered the University of Illinois at Champaign, where he again displayed intelligence and high motivation. He majored in engineering studies, studied French, and became active in student life. When the United States entered World War I in April 1917, Powell decided to enlist in the army. He served as a lieutenant in the 317th Engineers and the 365th Infantry Regiment, one of the segregated units in the U.S. Army. Assigned to the frontlines in France, he fell victim to a gas attack on the last day of the war. Powell escaped death, but his health was severely compromised.

Returning home, Powell went through a long period of recuperation. His health improved, allowing him to return to the University of Illinois, where he renewed his studies in electrical engineering. He graduated in 1922. While at Illinois, he met his wife, Lucille, with whom he had two children: a daughter, Bernardine, and a son, William J. Powell III. Diploma in hand, Powell returned to Chicago, where he became a successful businessman, running a chain of gas stations on the south side of Chicago in the 1920s.

Powell's interest in aviation dated back to the spring of 1927, when he happened to be in Paris at the time of Lindbergh's transatlantic flight. He was in the French capital for a meeting of the American Legion, which was celebrating the tenth anniversary of America's entry into World War I. The heroic nonstop flight of Lindbergh from New York to Le Bourget airport near Paris had been a global sensation, catapulting the young American aviator into fame and celebrity. While in Paris, Powell made a visit to Le Bourget and took his first airplane ride. Flying over the French capital proved to be an intoxicating experience for Powell, and he vowed to learn how to fly when he returned home.

The debut of the Bessie Coleman Aero Club in 1931 signaled a new phase in William Powell's life. The club quickly grew in numbers, attracting a large number of young people to flying. Powell insisted that the club be open to all races. He also took steps to recruit young women to aviation, organizing a five-member flying team called the Blackbirds. In 1931, this unique team of female fliers played a highly visible role in the club's first air show at the old Los Angeles East Side Airport. As their sponsor, Powell attempted to set up a special Hundred City Tour for the Blackbirds, but this plan never came to fruition due to a lack of funding. One notable member of the Blackbirds, Marie Dickerson Coker, was a dancer and vaudevillian, who acquired celebrity status at the Cotton Club in Los Angeles. Coker's motivation to join the Blackbirds was due, in part, to Powell's influence, who became her mentor in aviation matters. But Coker was caught up—as many were at the time—by the allure and excitement of flying; she confessed, too, that she found the aerial exploits of barnstormers and their stylish flying garb powerfully appealing. Coker viewed flying as another stage for performance. She took flying lessons at the Bessie Coleman Aero Club, where she was a member. However, the Blackbirds proved to be a short-lived phenomenon. After Powell failed to gain funding for a national tour, the group fell apart. The Blackbirds, and other club members, flew

LEFT William J. Powell Jr. took a keen interest in attracting black youth for the air age.

ABOVE William J. Powell Jr. gave the Los Angeles flying club a dynamic program of aeronautical instruction, flying lessons, and public outreach to all races.

RIGHT Members of the Los Angeles Flying Club, ca. 1934

FAR RIGHT Rare cockpit image of William J. Powell Jr. aloft over Southern California in the mid-1930s

in a variety of aircraft used by the club, including a Waco 10, an Alexander Eaglerock, and a Curtiss Wright Travelaire.

The success of the Bessie Coleman Aero Club's 1931 air show marked an important milestone. Powell had attended the National Air Races in 1929, an event that made a profound impression on him. He took great delight in the aerobatics performed by the two military demonstration teams, the navy's Three Sea Hawks and the army's Three Musketeers. This was the era of the open cockpit biplanes made of wood and fabric and often powered by modern and highly reliable radial engines. In the hands of a skilled pilot, these airplanes could perform remarkable aerobatic feats: flying loops, figure eights, stalls and spins, and high-speed passes over the crowds.

Powell felt that an all-black air show in Los Angeles would give the Bessie Coleman Aero Club new visibility, even as it offered a dramatic venue to reach out to the African American community in Los Angeles. Gaining the enthusiastic support of members of the club, he quickly organized the first all-black air show. Powell chose Sunday, December 6, 1931, to stage the event. Always attentive to the publicity, billboards were rented to promote what Powell called the first Colored Air Circus. The cost of admission was fifty cents for adults and twenty cents for children. The air show aimed to not only showcase the club's growing cadre of fliers, but also recruit African Americans, especially young people, to the cause of aviation.

The program for the air show gave top billing to the Blackbirds, but included a number of aerial performers. Powell joined two other licensed pilots, Irvin Wells and William Atkins, to form one demonstration flying team. Parachute jumpers Maxwell Love and Lottie Theodore also participated in the air show. The air show proved to be a great success, attracting some fifteen thousand people. The event concluded fittingly with the Goodyear blimp Volunteer appearing over the airfield and dropping a wreath in memory of Bessie Coleman.

During the early 1930s Powell discovered that flying posed certain challenges and occasional perils, especially on adventurous long-distance journeys. One key collaborator with Powell on these long-range flights was James Herman Banning. In many ways, Banning was the most experienced black flier in the country, a former barnstormer from Iowa and a skilled dedicated instructor for the apprentice pilots in Los Angeles. On one occasion, he flew from Los Angeles to San Diego with Powell and Marie Dickerson Coker to gain experience with navigation, using a compass and drift indicator.

COLORED AIR CIRCUS

FEATURING

"FIVE BLACKBIRDS" - ONLY COLORED AVIATORS WITH U.S. GOVERNMENT LICENSES!

COL. RUPERT JULIAN
WORLD FAMOUS COLORED AVIATOR

MARIE DAUGHTRY - CHUTE JUMPER
MARIE DICKERSON - AVIATRIX

MATTHEW J. CHAMPANA
"The Human Arrow"

FRANK SEBASTIAN'S COTTON CLUB ORCHESTRA & ENTERTAINERS DIRECTOR S LES HITE

Clarence Muse

LOS ANGELES EASTSIDE AIRPORT
800 EAST WHITTIER BLVD. - ½ MILE EAST OF MONTEBELLO

ADULTS 60¢

SUNDAY - DECEMBER 6TH

The trip went well outbound, but on the return flight at dusk they encountered fog. The more seasoned Banning took the controls and climbed above the fog, reaching an altitude of 4,500 feet. To their surprise, a blanket of clouds seemed to stretch to the horizon, obscuring the Pacific Ocean coastline—leaving no way to distinguish between the ground, the beach, or the ocean. Flying north above the clouds and toward Los Angeles, their fuel supply began to run low. With an estimated five minutes left, Banning flew a tight spiral through a hole in the clouds. Now above the ground and out of the fog, the engine shut down suddenly, creating a real emergency situation. Banning turned the plane into the wind and made a safe landing in an orange grove. Except for paying $25 for minor damage to two orange trees, the intrepid aviators and their airplane emerged relatively unscathed. On another outing, Powell and Banning flew over the desert in Baja California, where they were again forced to make an emergency landing. Isolated in the desert, it took them several days before they found their way to safety.

Powell occupies a special place in history as a prophet of aviation. He expressed great optimism that aviation would transform modern life—that this same modern technology would offer African Americans a unique avenue to escape racial segregation. The best ex-

Hubert Julian, one of the few licensed black pilots in Depression-era America, points to a billboard announcing the 1931 air show. The all-black air show, staged in Los Angeles, represented a milestone for William J. Powell Jr. and attracted an estimated fifteen thousand people. The air show followed the established pattern of aerobatics, stunts, and parachute jumps.

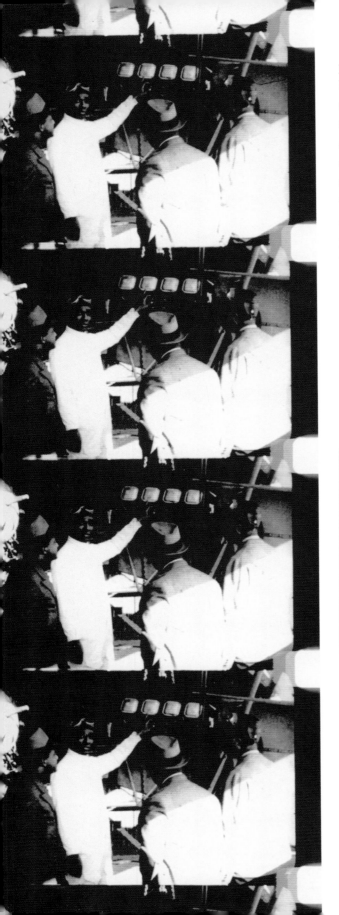

pression of his personal vision was his classic 1934 book *Black Wings*. The foreword to the book speaks directly to Powell's "all-consuming dream of filling the sky with skilled *black wings*." The book became a manifesto for blacks to join the new aeronautical world, to carve out careers as pilots, mechanics, and aviation industrialists. The book, at its heart, was an account of Powell's own personal odyssey in aviation. Powell wrote the book in an upbeat and positive way, suggesting that the future was filled with possibilities, especially jobs in aviation for black youth.

A tireless worker, Powell attempted a new strategy in the late 1930s. He organized a new entity under the name of Craftsmen of Black Wings. The official newsletter, *Craftsmen of Aero Wings* (1937–1938), was sent out to a small nationwide group of air enthusiasts. For the scattered and isolated black air enthusiasts, Powell's organization

ABOVE A major acquisition for the Los Angeles Flying Club was its own aircraft, which offered members a chance to take flying lessons and promote the work of *Black Wings*.

LEFT William J. Powell Jr. inspects his plane before a flight. Powell began his flying career in the late 1920s and soon emerged as an experienced aviator. He recorded his many aviation stories in his book *Black Wings*.

This cartoon of a black
youth dreaming of flying
appeared in William J. Powell
Jr.'s *Craftsman of Aero-
News*. Powell's Black Wings
organization gave special
attention to black youth in its
many promotional activities.

was a welcome clearinghouse of news and an excellent networking tool. The newsletter contained technical articles, editorials, news from around the world dealing with black aviators, and persistent appeals to raise scholarship money to send black youth to aeronautical schools. Powell used *Craftsmen of Aero Wings* to express his own vision of the future, which amounted to an elaborate blueprint for blacks to organize their own flight schools, businesses, and even airlines. Powell believed that such pioneering work would assist in breaking down the racial barriers of the era. Once blacks demonstrated their aptitude for flying, Powell argued, racial prejudice would subside. He actively appealed to black businessmen to become patrons. At one juncture, Powell recruited famed bandleader Duke Ellington and heavyweight boxer Joe Louis to endorse his Craftsmen of Black Wings organization. For Powell, the black church also became a key institution to offer legitimacy and concrete support.

Unfortunately, by the end of the 1930s, Powell had to abandon his promotional work. His health crisis, a result of injuries suffered in World War I, required him to retire from an active life. Powell spent his last years in a sanatarium. He died in 1942.

CHICAGO: THE CHALLENGERS

Chicago rivaled Los Angeles as an early center for black aviation. Here, too, a flying club, the Challenger Air Pilots Association, was organized in 1931. Two skilled pioneer pilots led the effort to build the fledgling new club: Cornelius Coffey and John C. Robinson. They would be joined in the decade of the 1930s by a talented group of air enthusiasts, which included Harold Hurd, Willa Brown, Bill Thompson, Chauncey Spencer, Dale White, Janet Bragg, and others. As their fellow enthusiasts in Los Angeles, Chicagoans looked upon Bessie Coleman as a source of inspiration.

Coffey, soft-spoken and determined, played a key role in inaugurating the Challenger Air Pilots' Association. Coffey was a skilled automotive mechanic, a man who found himself keenly interested in aviation after Lindbergh's extraordinary flight. He decided to apply to the Curtiss-Wright Aeronautical School, but was extremely frustrated when he was rejected on racial grounds. Coffey lobbied Curtiss-Wright persistently to train him and a special class of black students on a segregated basis. Coffey's main goal was to obtain the training, even if he had to tolerate the humiliation of racial segregation. In time, he established important personal milestones, earning licenses as a pilot and aircraft engine mechanic. He became a core leader for the Challenger Air Pilots' Association. His knowledge of technical matters served as a source of inspiration for other members of the African American community who wished to pursue work in aviation, or even qualify as pilots and/or engine mechanics.

In 1935, Fascist Italy, under Benito Mussolini, invaded Ethiopia. At the time, Ethiopia (also known as Abyssinia) was one of only two independent nations in Africa, with the rest of the continent still under colonial rule. The remote Ethiopian kingdom appealed to many blacks—ministers, writers, and community leaders—for its heroic resistance. Ethiopia possessed an ancient Christian civilization (one even predating England) and during its long history had resisted Muslim invaders, European colonialists, and—now in the twentieth century—Fascist Italy.

TOP Heavyweight boxing champion Joe Louis (*left*) visits William J. Powell Jr. (*right*) at this workshop in Los Angeles. Powell recruited the famous athlete to promote the activities of the Black Wings organization.

BOTTOM LEFT William J. Powell Jr. published *Craftsman of Aero-News* to promote his ambitious program of Black Wings. His national journal aimed to rally blacks to careers in aviation and combat racial prejudice in the United States.

BOTTOM RIGHT When William J. Powell Jr. reached out to the African American community he confidently forecast "one million jobs" in the new world of aviation. This became a most attractive, if visionary, prediction of new careers for black youth in the era of the Great Depression. Powell remained an optimist throughout his life.

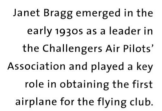

Janet Bragg emerged in the early 1930s as a leader in the Challengers Air Pilots' Association and played a key role in obtaining the first airplane for the flying club.

The plight of Ethiopia evoked deep sympathy within the African American community. Both the Los Angeles and Chicago flying clubs organized relief supplies for the embattled Haile Selassie. One of the first Americans to reach Ethiopia was Hubert Julian, who was eventually expelled for alleged collaboration with the Italians and wrecking one of the country's few airplanes. John C. Robinson also decided to seek out new flying opportunities in distant Africa, and flew with the Ethiopian air force. Once he reached Africa, Robinson vigorously opposed Julian's self-styled mission and eventually replaced him as the key adviser to the government on aviation matters. For a short time, Robinson flew sorties for the Ethiopians, mostly liaison and relief flights. Back in Chicago, the Challengers attempted to support Robinson by raising money and sending relief supplies to Africa.

Robinson's service in the Ethiopian war has remained shrouded in mystery, but there is evidence that he did make substantial contributions to the war effort as a courier pilot. When Ethiopia finally fell to the invading Italian armies, Robinson had to escape, a dangerous, but successful, undertaking. When he returned home to Chicago, he was greeted as the Brown Condor. His story received wide media coverage, especially in the black newspapers. Community leaders and the clergy took a keen interest in Robinson's exploits, inviting him to speak at churches and clubs in the city. There was a massive outdoor reception in Chicago, attracting an estimated twenty thousand people.

Robinson's newfound fame, however, did not translate into a new career of aviation in the United States, largely because of his extreme individualism and tendency to prompt controversy with other black aviators. As the years passed, he struggled to launch his own aviation school in Chicago or to seek out a teaching position at Tuskegee, but success eluded him. Finally, he returned to Ethiopia after World War II, where he spent his remaining years. He mobilized a small group technicians and educators to form the Ethiopian Air Force Training Program after 1945. He won the admiration of his African hosts for his selfless service to Ethiopia. Robinson stayed on after the war and established a small air service flying surplus DC-3 aircraft, which became the forerunner of the modern Ethiopian Air Lines. The Brown Condor was a pioneer and gifted black aviator, whose life ended in relative obscurity.

During the 1930s William Powell Jr. had expressed similar sympathy for Ethiopia. He and his small company of aviation enthusiasts in Los Angeles could offer little concrete assistance, but he made effective use of Ethiopia as a metaphor for the small community of black aviators. For his stage play to promote aviation, Powell deliberately chose the title *Let Ethiopia Spread Her Wings* to make a cultural link to Africa. He used the emotion-laden metaphor for a stage play and his celebrated book, *Black Wings*, which appeared in 1935.

While the international crisis surrounding Ethiopia had generated interest, most black pilots faced their own problems at home. Racial discrimination seemed to block the Challengers flying club at every turn in Depression America. Coffey and Robinson—notwithstanding their licenses and manifest skills—were routinely barred from flying at local Chicago airports. When they would manage to make long-distance flights, there was always a great deal of uncertainty about what sort of reception awaited them at unfamiliar airports. Whites viewed black pilots as novelties, and were surprised to see blacks involved with such modern technology. Coffey reported that a he had experienced discrimination often while flying to a

John C. Robinson, pictured here in Ethiopia, advised Emperor Haile Selassie on aviation matters. Robinson served in Ethiopia during the time of the Italian invasion in 1935. Later in life, Robinson helped to establish the first Ethiopian air lines.

strange airport where it was not unusual to be denied service or fuel because of his race.

Because of these realities, Coffey and Robinson decided to move the club and its small inventory of aircraft to a more welcoming spot—in this case, to the all-black township of Robbins outside of Chicago. The club gained access to an open farm field where they built an airstrip and a hangar. It may have been a primitive setting, but Robbins served as an improvised airport for the Challengers, where they could fly freely. In 1933, the Robbins experiment came to an abrupt end. A sudden windstorm swept through the area, toppling the club's improvised hangar and damaging the small number of parked aircraft. In the aftermath of the tragedy, Coffey—a man

ROBBIN'S AIRPORT (All Colored
Mgr. by J.C. ROBINSON 1/30/33
Headquarters of
CHALLENGER AERO CLUB

THORNTON STUDIOS
CHICAGO

highly respected in Chicago aviation circles—used his considerable diplomatic skills and personal contacts to seek out a new location. Finally, he made arrangements with the white owner of the Harlem Airport in Chicago to allow the club to set up shop at one end of the airfield. With this move, the Challengers club managed to stay alive, notwithstanding the limited funds and less than ideal circumstances.

The Challengers attracted a significant number of women to its flying program. Janet Harmon Bragg contributed funds to purchase an aircraft and took a keen interest in all aspects of the Challenger Air Pilots Association. Bragg was joined by Willa Brown. Influenced by the flamboyant style of the barnstormers, Brown decided to take on the style of these elite aviators, wearing white jodhpurs, leather jacket, and boots. She quickly emerged as the most visible representative of the Challengers. Enoch Waters, then city editor of the *Chicago Defender*, wrote in his memoirs of the day Willa Brown visited his newspaper: "She made such a stunning appearance that all the typewriters, which had been clacking noisily, suddenly went si-

The Challenger Air Pilots' Association became Chicago's first all-black flying club. Organized by John C. Robinson and Cornelius Coffey, the flying club built its first airstrip with its rudimentary hangar at Robbins, Illinois, in 1933.

Harold Hurd earned his pilot's license while a member of the Challengers flying club in Chicago. He later served as a sergeant in the U.S. Army Air Forces training program at Tuskegee in World War II.

RIGHT Earl W. Renfroe, a Chicago dentist, earned his pilot's license in 1934 and his transport license two years later. Renfroe is pictured in the cockpit of his Travel Air in 1937.

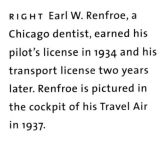

lent." That day, in the summer of 1936, the young Brown came to the *Chicago Defender,* one of America's major black newspapers, to promote an air show at Harlem airfield. She told Waters that there were "thirty of us," and requested publicity from the newspaper. Waters decided to attend the air show and even rode in a plane. In the years that followed, Waters reported regularly on the Challenger Air Pilots Association, becoming, in his own way, an aviation enthusiast and an advocate of the idea that the black community should be more involved in the new world of aviation.

The Chicago club possessed a unique vitality, attracting to its circle of active leaders a number of prominent local black professionals, such as Earl W. Renfroe, a dentist, and A. Porter Davis, a physician. The creation of the National Airmen's Association allowed for a wide range of individuals to support aviation in the black community. One interesting and highly visible way to promote the cause was to sponsor an air show. In the late 1930s, all-black air shows were popular in Chicago and in other parts of the country, often involving traveling barnstormers and death-defying aerial acts. Willie "Suicide" Jones attracted a wide following with his parachute jumps. In 1939, he attempted to break the existing world record from extreme altitude, a record then held by a Russian parachutist. Precise details on

WILLA BROWN VISITS THE
CHICAGO DEFENDER

Willa Brown became a well-known woman pilot in Chicago in the 1930s, playing a leadership role in the Challenger Air Pilots' Association.

"When Willa Brown, a young woman wearing white jodhpurs, jacket, and boots, strode into our newsroom in 1936, she made such a stunning appearance that all the typewriters, which had been clacking noisily, suddenly went silent. Unlike most first time visitors, she wasn't all all bewildered. She had such confident bearing and there was an undercurrent of determination in her voice.

"'I want to speak to Mr. Enoch Waters,' she said. I wasn't unhappy at the prospect of discovering who she was and what she wanted. I had an idea she was a model representing a new commercial product that she had been hired to promote. 'I'm Willa Brown,' she informed me, seating herself without being asked.

"In a businesslike manner she explained that she was an aviatrix and wanted some publicity for a Negro air show at Harlem Airport on the city's southwest side. Except for the colorful 'Colonel' Hubert Flauntleroy Julian, who had gained a lot of publicity for his exploits, and 'Colonel' John Robinson, a Chicago flyer who was in Ethiopia heading up Haile Selassie's air force, I was unaware of any other Negro aviators, particularly in Chicago.

"'There are about thirty of us,' she informed me, 'both men and women.' Most were students, she added, but several had obtained their licenses and one, Cornelius Coffey, was an expert aviation and engine mechanic who also held a commercial pilot's license and was a certified flight instructor. He was the leader of the group. She informed me that she had a limited commercial pilot's license.

"Fascinated both by her and the idea of Negro aviators, I decided to follow up the story myself. Accompanied by a photographer, I covered the air show. About 200 or 300 other spectators attended, attracted by a story in the *Defender*. So happy was Willa over our appearance that she offered to take me up for a free ride. She was piloting a Piper Cub, which seemed to me, accustomed as I was to commercial planes, to be a rather frail craft. It was a thrilling experience, and the maneuvers and stalls were exhilarating, though momentarily frightening. I wasn't convinced of her competence until we landed smoothly."

Enoch Waters
City Editor
Chicago Defender

Jones's career remain elusive, but the *Chicago Defender* did follow his aerial exploits, real and imagined, with keen interest, dubbing him the "Human Skyrocket." In the September 16, 1939 edition, the newspaper reported that the intrepid Jones had made a delayed parachute jump on August 28, 1938 from an altitude of 29,400 feet and delayed pulling his rip chord until he descended to 2,000 feet. This jump took place over Dixie Airport in Harvey, Illinois. Another leading black parachutist, Major George Fisher, described in an air show leaflet (1939) as the "Veteran Daredevil of Chicago," was scheduled to make a delayed parachute jump from 10,000 feet. Such aerial feats routinely aimed for the parachutist to land dramatically in front or near the grandstand filled with awe-struck onlookers. These aerial circuses, often called "Colored Air and Ground Shows," followed the same script as mainstream events, drawing large and enthusiastic crowds, but they were isolated and reflected the fact that aviation in America remained largely segregated during the years of the Great Depression.

Cornelius Coffey organized his own aeronautical school in the late 1930s, and this initiative gave the small black aviation community in Chicago an institutional basis that it had previously lacked. In 1939, Congress approved the establishment of the Civilian Pilot Training Program (CPTP), which aimed to train a pool of pilots in anticipation of any future national emergency. The program made funds explicitly available for traditionally black colleges. Tuskegee Institute, Howard University, and Hampton Institute received approval for on-campus CPTP programs. A real breakthrough came when Chicago's Coffey School received a franchise to organize a CPTP school, one of the few awarded to a proprietary organization. That same year, Coffey and others in the National Airmen's Association, along with the support of the *Chicago Defender*, sponsored a special flight to Washington, D.C., to lobby for racial equality in all federal aviation programs, and, in particular, the integration of the Army Air Corps. Two fliers from Chicago were chosen for the high-profile aerial trek: Dale L. White and Chauncey E. Spencer. The endeavor proved successful, resulting in a meeting between White and Spencer and then Missouri Senator Harry S. Truman.

The strides made by African American aviators in the 1930s were dramatic and relentless, establishing new benchmarks—most notably repudiating the myth that blacks lacked the aptitude to fly. Still, this small and scattered community of air enthusiasts remained on the periphery of the American aeronautical world. This situation was destined to change with the approach of World War II.

TOP Cornelius Coffey, who was a key leader in the Challengers Air Pilots' Association in Chicago, poses with a young woman air enthusiast.

BOTTOM Pioneer aviator Willa Brown (*center*) poses with Perry Young and his mother, Edith Young, at Chicago's Harlem Airport in the late 1930s. Young went on to be serve as a flight instructor at Tuskegee in World War II and a commercial pilot in the postwar years.

James Herman Banning gained fame as a barnstormer and transcontinental flyer until his untimely death in 1933 in a plane crash.

CHAPTER 3

LONG-DISTANCE FLYING

GETTING AIRBORNE DURING THE GREAT DEPRESSION was no easy task. In the 1930s, flight training was difficult to arrange, costly, and time-consuming. Even with training, newly minted black aviators often found themselves relegated to the periphery of America's aeronautical community. Such racial exclusion created a parallel world of flying—all-black flying clubs, air shows, and training programs. The main task for early black aviation pioneers was to break out of this pattern of segregation.

How to break the isolation? One highly visible avenue for black flyers was to establish new air records, in particular in the realm of duration flying. Long-distance flights attracted wide public attention. Some heroic pilots, particularly Charles Lindbergh and Amelia Earhart, had crossed continents and oceans on memorable aerial treks. Amy Johnson had flown from London to Australia. Soviet pilots had made two transpolar flights in the summer of 1937. Transcontinental flights were often important measures of air progress. Such flying was highly competitive and highly risky due to severe and shifting weather patterns, navigation challenges, and sudden engine breakdowns.

The interest of black pilots in duration flights arose in lock step with the establishment of the flying clubs. Based in Los Angeles, William Powell, for example, attempted several long-distance hops to San Diego, Baja California, and across mountains and deserts to Arizona. In Chicago, Cornelius Coffey and John Robinson attempted an arduous flight from Illinois to Tuskegee Institute in Alabama. Their goal was to appeal to the famed Tuskegee Institute to offer aviation training to blacks. The long journey to Tuskegee in the depths of the Depression was a costly affair for the pilots. The air trek included one mishap that seriously damaged their aircraft. Each venture out beyond the horizon in one of these open cockpit biplanes tested pilots, no matter how experienced they were: they had to demonstrate not only endurance, but also navigational skills and the ability to improvise in the face of frequent mechanical breakdowns along the way.

The most alluring goal was to complete the first transcontinental flight of the United States, alone or in a team. Once achieved, this aerial feat would give the struggling community of black aviators a new sense of legitimacy.

BANNING AND ALLEN: THE FIRST TRANSCONTINENTAL FLIGHT

James Herman Banning was one of the first African Americans to gain a pilot's license. He quickly established himself as a barnstormer and one of the most talented black aviators in the 1930s. His dream was to become the first black pilot to complete a transcontinental flight of the United States. As a youth, Banning enrolled in Iowa State to study electrical engineering, but soon left college to pursue his passion for flying. Tall and charismatic, Banning displayed a fierce determination to overcome the pervasive racism of the age to realize his goal of becoming a licensed pilot. Repeated efforts to gain entrance to formal programs of aeronautical training were met with rejection. Undaunted, he recruited a former army pilot, a veteran of World War I, to teach him how to fly. In May 1926, Banning finished his flight training and qualified as the first African American to obtain a pilot's license from the U.S. Department of Commerce. With this critical benchmark behind him, Banning decided to pursue a career in aviation, performing as a stunt pilot at air shows in the Midwest. The income was minimal, forcing the young black aviator to live on the edge of poverty. Finally, he decided to seek new opportunities and headed for Los Angeles in September 1929, where he joined William Powell's Bessie Coleman Aero Club.

In 1932, Banning decided the time had come for him to attempt a transcontinental flight. He felt he was ready, even overqualified for the endeavor with eight hundred hours of flying recorded in his flight log. In Los Angeles, Banning had emerged as a leading figure in the Bessie Coleman Aero Club. There was no other pilot in the club, with the possible exception of Powell, who possessed the experience and talent of Banning. No one doubted that Banning possessed the necessary flying skill for a cross-continental aerial trek, but there was considerable skepticism about the financial backing for his proposed flight. Banning did not own a plane and lacked the personal savings to finance his trip. The Bessie Coleman Aero Club, itself operating on a shoestring budget, could offer only moral support. Getting a transcontinental flight underway became a daunting task.

Banning scored a major breakthrough when an Alexander Eaglerock aircraft became available for his use. Arthur Dennis, a businessman in Los Angeles, had once dreamed of making a transcontinental flight, but decided that his airplane could be employed best by Banning in an "honest effort to aid negro progress." The Eaglerock, though used and weather-beaten, was nevertheless a fine flying machine. The Iowa barnstormer lost no time in refurbishing the loaned airplane, making repairs and upgrades to assure the veteran aircraft could fly the roundtrip journey from Southern California to New York. The Alexander Eaglerock was a two-place, open cockpit biplane fitted with a 100 hp engine. With its struts, wire bracing, and fixed landing gear, the plane lacked any effective streamlining. It was constructed of wood and fabric and, for its time, was considered an excellent civilian aircraft. Private pilots admired the plane for its maneuverability, sturdy construction, and general reliability. The Eaglerock, however, was an austerely equipped craft, being fitted only with the minimal instrumenta-

J. Herman Banning's airplane Miss Ames. Banning, seated in rear cockpit, flew the biplane during his barnstorming days in Iowa in the early 1930s.

RIGHT Another view of Miss Ames with Banning in the cockpit. Banning earned his pilot license in the early 1930s and then emerged as one of the most prominent black stunt pilots.

tion. In the 1930s, a pilot could use an altimeter and compass to gauge height and direction, but there was little else, and no radio. If slow, the biplane could land and take off on short runways, and, in emergencies, the pilot could easily land the plane on a road or in an open field. Banning considered the Eaglerock to be ideal for his purposes. Though lacking in high-speed performance, the plane offered a steady (and hopefully reliable) passage across the United States.

Once he secured the aircraft, Banning turned his attention to the critical matter of financing the trip. In *Black Wings*, Powell recorded how Banning worked out his financing and recruited a flying companion for the journey. After several failed overtures to local businessmen, Banning had a conversation with Thomas Cox Allen, an employee at Douglas Aircraft Company in California, who offered to come up with an advance payment for fuel, oil, and other expenses

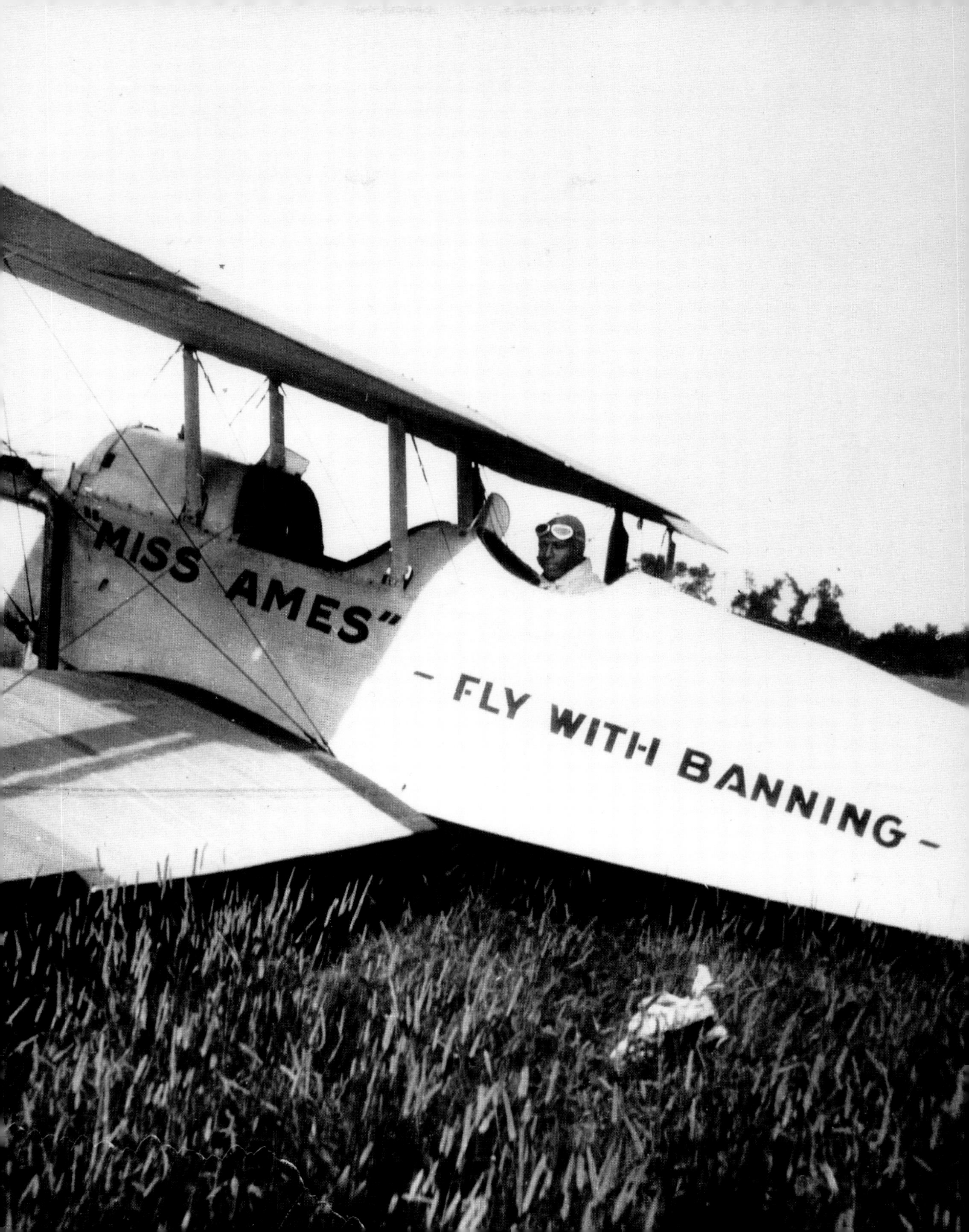
"MISS AMES"
- FLY WITH BANNING -

if he could join Banning as a mechanic. When Banning told Allen that his money offer fell short of covering the entire expenses for the transcontinental flight, it appeared that the deal had fallen through. The irrepressible Allen then suggested they pay for the journey by seeking out contributions from black churches and sympathetic patrons along the way: "We'll be just like hobos, begging our way." Banning reacted positively to Allen's bold idea: "Fine," he replied, "That gives me an idea. We will capitalize on our flight. We'll call ourselves the 'Flying Hobos.'"

Thomas Allen was a loner and not necessarily a highly respected figure within the small black aviation community in Los Angeles. For Powell and others in the club, Allen was a self-promoter at heart, a man who had made his appearance only in the eleventh hour. From their perspective, there were worthier individuals in the club who should have accompanied Banning on his historic flight. Allen was born in Texas, grew up in Oklahoma, and moved to Los Angeles in 1929. As a youth, Allen had become enamored with aviation, dreaming of qualifying as both a pilot and mechanic. While real job possibilities in aviation remained elusive for Allen, he had managed to acquire some experience in aircraft engine repair.

When Banning and Allen departed from Dyce Airport in Los Angeles, it was rumored that they had only $25 in cash between them, having used most of Allen's savings to outfit and fuel the Eaglerock. The first leg of the journey was to nearby Arlington airport where they landed and stayed overnight. For the flight across the United States, Banning selected a route that traversed Arizona, New Mexico, and Texas, to be followed by a northeasterly heading across the plains to the Midwest, and finally through Pennsylvania and New Jersey to their New York destination. Except for the American Southwest, the itinerary assured that the Flying Hobos would be close to major population centers along the flight path.

The first major benchmark for Banning and Allen was their passage through the San Jacinto Range, the San Bernardino Mountains, and the San Gorgonio Pass en route to Yuma, Arizona. The local airport manager in Yuma remembered Banning and, as a token of support, filled the plane's gas tank. The next day, the men were off to El Paso, going through the Apache Pass and around the Franklin Mountains. Departing the municipal airport at El Paso, Banning steered the Eaglerock toward Midland, Texas. While flying around El Capitan Peak, they had to climb to an altitude of 9,000 feet, where they encountered heavy clouds, fog, and rain. Banning flew blind for

J. Herman Banning
Pilot

Thomas C. Allen
Mec.

to by Johnson PS, Pa.

FIRST TRANS-CONTINENTAL FLIGHT

periods of time. They made it through this gauntlet of bad weather and pressed on to Wink, Texas, where they stayed for the night. At this juncture, the Eaglerock had safely transported the intrepid aviators over mountains and desert, passing through no fewer than four states.

The next morning, with heavy clouds still hovering over them, Banning and Allen headed for Wichita Falls, confident that the worst weather was now behind them. They reached Wichita Falls in the late afternoon, and decided to stay over night. Throughout the trip, Banning always elected to reach a destination by dusk, unwilling to fly in twilight over unfamiliar territory. Whenever they landed, Banning and Allen created a sensation; for the locals, as with most Americans, black aviators were a novelty—and their quest to fly across the country struck the locals as an extraordinary undertaking, especially in such a derelict aircraft. More often than not, they were greeted with curiosity rather than open hostility.

Keeping the aircraft fueled and their stomachs full was no easy task. While in New Mexico, Allen sold his watch to raise needed

One of the first major milestones was the Banning and Allen transcontinental flight of 1932. Flown in an *Alexander Eaglerock*, the historic flight inaugurated a series of long-range flights by black aviators. The team called themselves the Flying Hobos, because they raised financial backing along the way to complete their transcontinental flight.

funds so they could continue the journey. The black churches they encountered along the way routinely offered assistance, but not necessarily on a lavish scale. At one church, for example, the sympathetic pastor sent around the collection plate and managed to raise eleven dollars, not a huge amount, but enough to keep them airborne for a day. Banning routinely inscribed the names of individual contributors on the wing of the Eaglerock. One major white contributor was oil businessman William Skelly, who paid the fuel bill for the leg from Tulsa to St. Louis.

While the Eaglerock proved to be a reliable aircraft, there was one serious mechanical mishap on the approach to St. Louis. While in flight and cruising in a steady fashion, Banning detected an engine malfunction—the 100 hp engine began to sputter and lose power, the propeller spinning aimlessly and slowly in the wind. This event compelled Banning to make an emergency landing. The descent to earth was executed with finesse, without any damage to the aircraft or injury to the crew. Finding a way to repair the aircraft engine appeared to be a daunting task; they were in a strange place and with no substantial funds to repair or replace the engine. Aid eventually came from a local trade school where the white students rushed to assist the black fliers. They discovered that only minor repairs were necessary, but the tired Eaglerock engine required a specific part that could only be found on a 1928 Nash automobile. The fliers with the students searched a local junkyard and retrieved the desired part. The Flying Hobos were airborne once again.

As Banning and Allen progressed across the country, they caught the attention of various black-owned newspapers. The *Chicago Defender*, for example, took a keen interest in the pioneering flight, alerting its readership—and the larger African American community—to the pioneering character of the flight. Other newspapers followed. This sort of coverage had a substantial influence on the success of the transcontinental journey. Contributions started to increase. There was also the sheer excitement over the bold flight and hopes expressed that Banning and Allen would make it cross country in their *Eaglerock* airplane.

Slowly, Banning and Allen edged their way over the Midwest states and toward the still distant target of Long Island. They departed St. Louis and made excellent progress as they crossed Illinois farm country, Terre Haute, Indiana, and Columbus, Ohio. One key geographical reference point was old Route 40, which meandered through these states. While following the highway eastbound out of Columbus, they encountered some engine trouble again, this time near the small city of Cambridge. When the engine stopped abruptly, Banning made a controlled descent toward a cow pasture, passing over fences and around trees. Upon reaching the ground safely, Banning remarked, "You don't die every time your motor does. Sure we are going to sleep under the wings tonight. It won't be the first time." The stop in Cambridge, as it turned out, was short-lived; repairs were made quickly and the Eaglerock was airborne once again.

The next stop at Pittsburgh received considerable publicity. At this juncture, the *Pittsburgh Courier*, the local black newspaper with a national readership, had paved the way for their arrival with sustained news coverage. A group of local dignitaries, led by R. L. Vann, the editor of the *Pittsburgh Courier*, greeted the transcontinental fliers. Vann arranged for Banning and Allen to raise additional funds by joining Franklin Delano Roosevelt's presidential campaign. The fliers were hired to drop some fifteen thousand leaflets as they moved eastward across Pennsylvania, targeting the cities of Johnstown, Harrisburg, and Philadelphia.

On October 9, 1932, Banning and Allen reached Valley Stream Airport on Long Island, New York, bringing to a close a twenty-two day transcontinental saga. The actual flying time had been forty-one hours, which represented an important first for black aviators. The mainstream press, for the most part, had ignored the flight, but the black press had done an excellent job of showcasing it. New York City gave Banning and Allen an enthusiastic welcome. They made the rounds in the black community, visited nightclubs, and met celebrities Duke Ellington and Cab Calloway. Even Mayor Jimmy Walker gave the two fliers the key to the city, a token of appreciation for their aerial triumph.

Plans for the return flight proved to be ill-fated: the Eaglerock crashed in Pennsylvania, just hours after Banning and Allen took off on their return trip. The damage to the aircraft was substantial, and eliminated any chance of a quick repair. There were no available funds to purchase another aircraft, so both fliers had to take the bus back to Los Angeles. Tragically, James Herman Banning died in a plane crash the following year. Thomas Allen lived until 1989, never realizing his ambitious dream of becoming a famous aviator. At one point, in the 1940s, he attempted to raise money for a round-the-world flight, but the project never came to fruition.

TOP Albert E. Forsythe and C.
Alfred Anderson consult their
map near Wichita, Kansas, en
route to the West Coast on
their transcontinental flight
in 1933.

CENTER Commemorative
envelope, dated September
23, 1933, "Newark Welcomes
Dr. Albert Forsythe and
C. Alfred Anderson, First
Transcontinental Flyers."

BOTTOM Anderson and
Forsythe christened their
Fairchild 24 airplane, the
Pride of Atlantic City. The
team reached Los Angeles
in July 1933 in the first
leg of their roundtrip
transcontinental flight.

THE ANDERSON-FORSYTHE SAGA

C. Alfred Anderson and Albert E. Forsythe occupy a special place in long-distance flight history. As a flying team, they established an exemplary record, completing the first roundtrip transcontinental flight on July 28, 1933 and conducting a far-ranging demonstration flight from the United States to the Caribbean the following year. Unlike Banning and Allen, the Anderson-Forsythe flights were well-financed and expertly publicized in advance. In light of the difficulties of the Depression era, the Anderson-Forsythe achievement stood out as a remarkable triumph; they excelled beyond all expectations and set a new standard for black pilots.

Anderson had displayed extraordinary boldness in seeking out a career in aviation. He possessed a strong personal drive to achieve and demonstrated impressive skills as a pilot. As a youth, he aspired to become a pilot, but discovered that blacks were barred from aeronautical flight training programs. Anderson saved his money, bought his own airplane, and hired a flight instructor to provide personal training. Shortly thereafter, he passed all the tests and qualified for a pilot's license from the Department of Commerce. By 1932, Anderson was the only African American who possessed a transport pilot license, which was then the highest pilot rating given by the Department of Commerce. With such a license, Anderson could hire himself out as a flight instructor or transport pilot.

Forsythe, a wealthy physician and businessman from Atlantic City, New Jersey, organized the National Negro Aeronautical Society to encourage blacks to enter aviation. Forsythe was a genuine air enthusiast; he had qualified for a private pilot's license, one of an estimated ten blacks listed by the Department of Commerce in 1932. However, Forsythe was more comfortable in his role as a patron, generously providing his own funds to promote worthy projects. He enjoyed flying immensely and sought out ways to promote airmindedness in the African American community.

Anderson teamed up with Forsythe in 1932 to plan a transcontinental flight. As events unfolded, Banning and Allen would achieve this distinction first, but Forsythe wanted to replicate the flight in a more substantial way by flying a roundtrip itinerary. He was convinced that aviation feats offered a powerful tool to break down racial prejudice. He gained the backing of the mayor and Chamber

NEWARK

WELCOMES

DR. ALBERT FORSYTHE

AND

C. ALFRED ANDERSON

FIRST TRANSCONTINENTAL NEGRO FLYERS

SEPTEMBER 23rd, 1933

NEGRO AERO. RECEPTION COMMITTEE.
J. B. JOHNSON, Chairman
W. E. BANKS, Vice-Chairman

OGDEN SHOEMAKER
424 ATLANTIC AVE
OCEAN CITY N.J.

PRIDE of ATLANTIC CITY

ATLANTIC CITY LOS ANGELES SAN FRANCISCO NEW YORK

NC 1267

The transcontinental
flyers are shown together
prior to their historic
flight from Atlantic City to
Los Angeles in 1933.

of Commerce of Atlantic City for the transcontinental flight. He
purchased a late model Fairchild high wing monoplane for the pro-
jected cross-country trip. He dubbed the plane The Pride of Atlantic
City. As with all his endeavors, Forsythe was an able and a clever
promoter, always seeking out the widest scope of support within and
beyond the black community.

On July 17, 1933, Anderson and Forsythe, with the blessing of
their Atlantic City sponsors, departed for Los Angeles. There were
some frustrating moments on the long trip, especially in the open-
ing hours when heavy fog over Camden, New Jersey, forced the team

to make an emergency landing. Once the fog lifted, they were off again, flying to Harrisburg where they stopped to refuel. Unlike Banning and Allen, there was no need to seek out contributions from locals: with their ample funds, Anderson and Forsythe could concentrate solely on flying. They pressed on in the summer of 1933, passing through a sequence of cities, typically on schedule: Pittsburgh, Columbus, Indianapolis, St. Louis, Kansas City, Wichita, Amarillo, Albuquerque, Winslow, and Kingman. At each stop, Anderson and Forsythe connected with local black leaders to promote their goodwill flight. The black newspapers also took an interest in their roundtrip transcontinental flight. Only once on the long trek did the fliers encounter any mechanical difficulty; at one remote spot in the American Southwest called Baldy Mesa, they discovered that the Fairchild engine had overheated, so they decided to land temporarily.

When the Anderson and Forsythe team finally reached Grand Central Airport in Los Angeles, they encountered an enthusiastic crowd of well wishers, a demonstration of local support organized by the irrepressible William Powell. There were representatives from many parts of the African American community in Southern California: Percy Buck from the Elks Lodge, labor leader Clarence Johnson, Floyd C. Covington of the Urban League, Reverend Harry Grant representing the local clergy, and many figures from the local business elite. Representatives from the Associated Negro Press and the *Pittsburgh Courier* reflected the attention of the print media in the event. Even Clarence Muse, a noted black motion picture and radio personality of the era, came to the airport to greet Anderson and Forsythe. The celebrities were joined by a large crowd of onlookers, who came to the airport out of curiosity. For Powell, the occasion had great symbolic meaning, calling to mind the image evoked by his play *Ethiopia Spreads Her Wings*. The metaphor of Ethiopia spreading her wings, in Powell's mind, became a dramatic way to suggest that African American fliers had achieved an important new milestone.

When they arrived, Anderson buzzed the field twice before he landed the Fairchild and taxied to the reception area. Powell described "noisy frenzy" unfolding. In *Black Wings*, he recorded an outburst of yells, auto horns, and thunderous applause. The press of the crowd, to Powell's alarm, pushed against the fence barrier: "Then there was a mad rush. Cameras clicked. Everybody tried to get close enough to get a good glimpse of these men. Children were

trampled in the mad rush. Women fainted. It took . . . nearly an hour to get the crowd back and quieted long enough to carry through the welcoming ceremony . . ." A banquet in the city followed the tumultuous arrival ceremony. Later, the mayor of Los Angeles, Frank Shaw, greeted the transcontinental pilots.

After a brief interlude, Anderson and Forsythe departed Los Angeles on July 21 for home; they reached Atlantic City on July 28, 1933, where they again received a warm welcome and widespread publicity for the completion of the first roundtrip transcontinental flight by black pilots. The civic leaders of Atlantic City presented the men with a special award.

The following year, Anderson and Forsythe were prepared for an even more ambitious undertaking—a Pan-American Goodwill Flight. For this high-risk flight to South America and the Caribbean, they planned to fly a brand new Lambert Monocoupe, which they named the Booker T. Washington in honor the famed black educator. To gain the widest support in the black community, Anderson and Forsythe flew the new airplane to the Tuskegee Institute where President Robert R. Moton would preside over the christening ceremony, which garnered considerable local press interest. The Goodwill Fliers landed the Lambert Monocoupe at a spacious golf course near the campus to accommodate the many interested onlookers. Always attentive to building a broad coalition of support, Forsythe organized the Inter-Racial Goodwill Aviation Committee to oversee and sponsor the flight. The aim of the fliers was not just to showcase the skill of black airmen, but also to enhance racial understanding.

The itinerary for the Goodwill Flight, by the standards of the day, was bold and far-reaching. The initial leg of the journey was a flight from Miami to Nassau, which would be the first flight ever made by a land plane to the island. The subsequent stops included Havana, Jamaica, Haiti, the Dominican Republic, Puerto Rico, the Virgin Islands, Grenada, Trinidad, and British Guiana. The arduous flight plan called for many hours of flying over the ocean and demanded skillful navigation by the two airmen. They would be flying in a small single-engine aircraft and be compelled to operate out of primitive airfields on several of their island stops. In many ways, the challenges faced on the Goodwill Flight dwarfed those encountered on the earlier transcontinental trek.

Anderson and Forsythe's island hopping proved to be carefree for the most part, except for one incident in their flight out of Port au Prince, Haiti, for Santo Domingo. The flight called for a long passage

TOP Anderson and Forsythe begin their 1934 Pan-American Goodwill Flight. The initial leg called for a flight from Miami to Nassau. The bold aerial journey to the Caribbean islands attracted considerable publicity.

BOTTOM For their Pan-American Goodwill Flight of 1934, Anderson and Forsythe flew a Lambert Monocoupe, dubbed the Spirit of Booker T. Washington. Robert R. Moton (*left*) is shown with Anderson and Forsythe at the time of the aircraft's christening.

Anderson and Forsythe are greeted by the governor of the Bahamas (*left*) on their 1934 Goodwill Flight.

across the island from Haiti in the west to the Dominican Republic in the east. After about a half hour into the flight, on November 20, 1934, as they crossed the Haitian-Dominican border, one of the valve stems in the Lambert Monocoupe's engine snapped, causing an engine failure. Anderson turned the aircraft around and guided it to a safe landing near Lake Enriquillo. The men felt relieved to have made a safe landing in the emergency—with no damage to the plane, but they were in a remote area, at least six miles from the nearest village. Even as they sought to make contact with the airport in Santo Domingo, the Dominican air force had launched a search for the Americans when their aircraft had not landed on schedule. Throughout the Goodwill Flight, the American State Department had offered assistance to the fliers and now worked with the Dominican government to locate them. Poor visibility hampered the search effort, but eventually Anderson and Forsythe were thrilled to see the arrival of the rescue party. The aircraft engine was repaired soon after and the tour resumed.

Wherever Anderson and Forsythe landed, they encountered a warm reception. One dramatic moment occurred on the initial flight to Nassau, when the fliers landed the Booker T. Washington at night on a dirt road illuminated by automobile lights. This particular bit of derring-do evoked great curiosity among the inhabitants. At the time, the island did not have an airport for land-based planes, so the Anderson-Forsythe arrival created a local sensation. At the St. Thomas, Virgin Islands, reception, the flyers put the Monocoupe down on the same golf course used by Charles Lindbergh seven years before. The governor greeted the visiting Americans and introduced them to the local dignitaries in a special reception. More than two thousand students from the local schools gathered to greet the fliers. On certain occasions, the fliers put on an impromptu air show, buzzing the assembled onlookers and putting the Booker T. Washington through aerial maneuvers.

At the end of the 1934 Goodwill Flight, both aviators took great pride in their remarkable achievement. They had completed an arduous itinerary of flying to distant places in the Caribbean Sea, made landings on primitive fields, overcame a serious engine failure and subsequent emergency landing, and fulfilled their overall purpose of promoting racial harmony.

What had been most remarkable about the long-distance flyers was their modest financial support. Banning and Allen, as they aptly described themselves, were flying hobos. Forsythe, a medical doctor of some means, had teamed with Anderson to make their flying a reality—Forsythe's willingness to subsidize the flights had been a crucial factor. For all black aviation enthusiasts in the Depression era, there was a keen sense of going it alone—no government subsidies and no patrons with deep pockets to rush to their aid.

Three cadets in the 1943 War Training Service (WTS) at the Coffey School of Aeronautics in Chicago stand next to a Waco aircraft. *Left to right*: Edward Gibbs, Henri Fletcher, and Charles Smallwood.

CHAPTER 4

IN THE SHADOW OF WAR

As the 1930s drew to a close, there was renewed pressure for the integration of the American armed forces. This reform movement gained momentum even as World War II engulfed Europe and threatened the United States. One of the major civil rights leaders to speak out was labor leader A. Philip Randolph, who headed the Brotherhood of Sleeping Car Porters. Randolph became an articulate and forceful advocate for change, a man keenly interested in ending racial discrimination in all spheres of American life. He became a powerful voice for allowing blacks to train as pilots and ground crew specialists in the U.S. Army Air Corps. The idea quickly won the support of other black leaders, most notably Walter White, the head of the NAACP. Black newspapers across the nation also joined the chorus demanding change. The air corps, however, stubbornly refused to remove the racial ban, still arguing that blacks, as a race, lacked the essential aptitude to fly. For the small number of blacks who did gain entry into the military in those days, for the army or the navy, it meant relegation to menial or unskilled labor. No blacks were admitted to the officer corps, except in segregated units. Not surprisingly, the American military mirrored the Jim Crow mentality of the era. One African American aviation pioneer, William J. Powell Jr., had attempted to gain entrance into the army flight training as early as the 1920s, only to be denied. His rejection had not been isolated or an aberration.

African Americans had volunteered for military service throughout the history of the United States, serving in the Revolutionary War, the Civil War, the Spanish-American War, and World War I. By the 1920s, a fixed pattern had emerged, one of segregation and service in nontechnical roles. There had been four historically all-black regiments in the United States Army: the 9th and 10th Cavalries and the 24th and 25th Infantries, supplemented by other units in the National Guard. Racial policies for the U.S. Army Air Corps had been influenced by the 1925 study "The Use of Negro Manpower in War." This report explicitly embraced racism, insisting that blacks were inferior, lacked intelligence and initiative, and possessed traits that disqualified them for leadership positions, especially where they would command white personnel. In fact, there were relatively few blacks in the army in the mid-1930s, less than 2 percent of the total of 360,000 men.

The year 1939 recorded some important new strides for racial equality. Out of Chicago, Chauncey Spencer with Dale White made an important demonstration flight to remind Americans that blacks were anxious to assert their proper role in the new world of aviation. The Spencer-White flight involved a highly publicized aerial trek to Washington, D.C., one dedicated to prove that negroes could fly. Spencer and White rented a Lincoln-Paige biplane for their flight, which included stops in ten cities. Upon reaching the nation's capital, both men participated in a spirited campaign to lobby Congress for an end to racial exclusion in the military. Spencer and White were sponsored by the National Airmen's Association and a host of civil rights leaders. Black newspapers, including the *Chicago Defender*, worked tirelessly to cover the flight and support its aims to end racial segregation in both civil and military aviation. The flight became an occasion for a concerted lobbying effort by the Spencer-

Benjamin O. Davis Jr.
graduated from West
Point in 1936. He served
in the infantry prior to his
assignment to Tuskegee.

White team to encourage Congress to end racial discrimination in the United States.

That same year, Congress had established the Civil Pilot Training Program (CPTP). This legislation became a morale builder for the small community of aspiring black pilots. While the CPTP legislation represented an important breakthrough in allowing blacks to participate in a federally funded flight training program, it mirrored in many ways the Jim Crow practices of the era: blacks could participate, but only on a segregated basis. A number of all-black colleges—for example, Hampton Institute, Howard University, and Tuskegee Institute—participated in the CPTP, helping to increase the number of licensed black pilots in the country. Cornelius Coffey, an experienced black aviation pioneer in Chicago, became one of

the few individuals to gain a franchise for CPTP program. At the time, Coffey operated one of the few successful black-owned flight schools. Coffey with other aviators such as Willa Brown helped to organize the National Airmen's Association. The Army Air Corps, however, refused to accept graduates from Coffey's flying school or, for that matter, any of the black trainees in the university-based CPTP programs.

By 1940, the Department of Commerce took note of the growing number of licensed black pilots, in the "Negro Statistical Bulletin No. 3." It was noted that at this time there were 231 black aviators listed by the Civil Aeronautics Administration (CAA). This listing included several categories of pilot licenses—for example, commercial, transport, private, student, and so on. In 1936, the number of licensed black pilots in all categories was merely forty-seven. The slight increase of licensed black pilots, the CAA concluded, was the result of CPTP programs at several black colleges and universities.

The approach of the 1940 presidential election created a heated context in which to demand the end of racism in the American military. President Franklin D. Roosevelt was seeking an unprecedented third term. His opponent was the popular Republican candidate Wendell Wilkie. Roosevelt needed the black vote. A. Philip Randolph pressed Roosevelt to make some concrete reforms in government contracts related to industry and racial policies in the military. With the boom in defense industries, Randolph and other civil rights leaders wanted fair and equal employment practices. In the military, they demanded the formal end to racial exclusion in the Army Air Corps, then an elite branch of the military. In the fall of 1940, Randolph, joined by Walter White, met with FDR to press the case for outlawing discrimination. Roosevelt expressed support, if cautiously. Certain changes did follow in 1940 and 1941, signaling a new era: Executive Order 8802 ended racial discrimination in hiring for defense industries and the War Department decreed that blacks could be admitted to training in the Army Air Corps. The draft had been instituted in the fall of 1940 and Roosevelt appointed William Hastie to serve as a civilian aide to the Secretary of War on issues related to the black community.

The decision to admit blacks to the Air Corps became known as the "experiment"—cheered by civil rights advocates and greeted by the army as an unwelcome departure from established tradition. The army, however, made it clear that the new program of flight training

TOP On a stopover at New York's Floyd Bennett Field in May 1939, Chauncey E. Spencer visits with his sister, Alroy Spencer Rivers.

BOTTOM A CPT flight instructor discusses a flying maneuver with a student at the Coffey School of Aeronautics in Chicago. The CPT program opened flight training to women cadets.

Flight instructor briefs cadets with maps at Tuskegee Army Air Field

A CPT class in aviation mechanics conducted at the Coffey School of Aeronautics, 1941. Offered at Chicago's Wendell Phillips High School, the class was open to all races.

A group of students at the Coffey School of Aeronautics gather with their instructor next to a Waco UPF-7 trainer.

for blacks would be conducted on a segregated basis. The Tuskegee Institute in Alabama, the famed school organized by Booker T. Washington, was selected as the site for a new army flight school. In March 1941, the first black cadets were accepted into the unprecedented flight training program. Tuskegee Army Air Base was formally established in July 1941. It became a unique entity in the Air Corps, set aside for the training of black pilots under the leadership of white officers. The first class consisted of thirteen cadets. By the time of the Japanese attack on Pearl Harbor later that year—the event that brought the United States into World War II—Tuskegee Army Air Field (TAAF) was in full stride. It would take a long time, however, for the so-called Tuskegee "experiment" to win acceptance in the American military.

Many black civil rights leaders, including William Hastie, criticized the segregated character of the Tuskegee flight program, seeing it as a continuation of Jim Crow policies. The NAACP and the black press echoed the same complaint. The creation of an all-black flying air unit, measured against past policies, represented a milestone. However, the implementation of the new program faced severe obstacles in 1941 and 1942, when the first white commanders of the air base displayed a thinly disguised hostility to the TAAF program. It was one thing to set up a pilot training program at Tuskegee, but it was a daunting task to train other personnel for the all black flying unit—in particular armament, engine, and maintenance specialists. These essential technicians had to be sent to far off Air Corps bases for training, which routinely sparked racial tensions. It became a nightmare to organize what amounted to a separate black air force within the Air Corps.

One key factor in setting the stage for success at Tuskegee was the appointment of Lieutenant Colonel Noel Parrish as base commander. Parrish was an experienced Air Corps pilot and instructor. Prior to his assignment to Tuskegee, he had met Cornelius Coffey in Chicago and felt sympathetic to the cause of allowing blacks to fly in the military. Short in stature, Parrish was an effective leader, winning the confidence of his white instructors and black cadets. He was affable and fair-minded, taking steps to integrate many aspects of life at the Tuskegee base. He maintained the highest standards for his black cadets, believing that sustained high standards assured success for the Tuskegee flight program. Since Tuskegee was a remote place he took steps to build morale, inviting to the air field many black celebrities—a group that included Lena Horne, Joe Louis, Ella

First Lady Eleanor Roosevelt worked tirelessly to promote racial equality and the full participation of African Americans in aviation, civil and military. She is shown here on a visit to Tuskegee, where she took a plane ride around the training facilities with Charles A. "Chief" Anderson at the controls.

A flight instructor in the advanced program at Tuskegee briefs cadets for a long-distance flight.

Fitzgerald, Louis Armstrong, and Langston Hughes, among others. Throughout the war years, Parrish walked a tightrope, overseeing the training of black aviators and representing the all-black flight program to the War Department in Washington, D.C.

The training at Tuskegee followed the established Air Corps practice of three phases: primary, basic, and advanced. The initial phase allowed black instructors, including C. Alfred Anderson to participate as an instructor. Anderson would garner more than forty thousand hours in the course of his long career. Given his long association with Tuskegee Institute, he had worked tirelessly in the prewar years to forge a viable CPTP program at the all-black school. By 1941, he was accepted as one of a handful of black instructors at the newly established TAAF. Anderson played a highly visible role in the primary phase of training the first Tuskegee class of cadets (Class 42-C). During the war years he acquired the affectionate name of "Chief Anderson" and was recognized as a key figure in the training of the Tuskegee airmen.

Linkwood Williams, a civilian
flight instructor, at the
Tuskegee Army Air Field in
World War II.

Chief Anderson played a dramatic role in promoting the TAAF
in 1941, when First Lady Eleanor Roosevelt visited the training facility. She had played a key role in advocacy of racial equality in 1940,
encouraging her husband, President Roosevelt, to approve flight
training for blacks in the Army Air Corps. She visited Tuskegee in
1941. And on this occasion she conducted a high profile review of
the aviation program, then in its start-up phase. To the surprise of
her Secret Service escorts, the First Lady requested a plane ride over
the Tuskegee flight training facilities. Chief Anderson, being one of
the most experienced instructors, then took the White House guest
aloft in a small Cub Trainer. The impromptu plane ride proved to be
an exhilarating experience for Eleanor Roosevelt. No less important,

ABOVE Black airmen went through a rigorous program of physical training at Tuskegee.

RIGHT Lieutenant Colonel Noel F. Parrish served as commander at the Tuskegee Army Air Field from 1942 to 1945. His inspired leadership was crucial for the success of the "Tuskegee experiment."

LEFT In 1942, Charles A. "Chief" Anderson had his pilot's license, which he had earned in the prewar years, renewed. Anderson served at Tuskegee as a primary flight instructor. Prior to his assignment at Tuskegee, he had logged more than 3,500 hours in the air.

BELOW The first class of black cadets for the U.S. Army Air Corps, Tuskegee Army Air Field, 1942

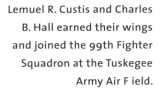
Lemuel R. Custis and Charles B. Hall earned their wings and joined the 99th Fighter Squadron at the Tuskegee Army Air F ield.

her willingness to fly with a black instructor at the TAAF sent a message of confidence to those engaged with the Tuskegee program. Her memorable plane ride carried great symbolic value. Throughout the war years, Eleanor Roosevelt became a reliable and vocal supporter of blacks in military aviation.

During the early months of the Tuskegee flight program there were only a handful of aircraft trainers available, a mere six PT-13s, four BT-13s, and four advanced AT-6s. Later this small flotilla would be expanded dramatically and include P-40 fighters. The initial goal was to train a cadre of black pilots to compose the new 99th Pursuit (later Fighter) Squadron. The 99th would be expanded and trained for overseas duty, and was assigned to the North African theater of

The first group o f black cadets to earn their wings at the Tuskegee Army Air Field gather along side a Vultee BT-13 trainer. *Left to right*: Lemuel R. Custis, Mac Ross, Benjamin O. Davis Jr., George S. Roberts, and Charles H. DeBow.

operations in 1943. A year later, further expansion of the TAAF set the stage for the organization of three additional fighter squadrons; these air units were deployed to Italy to form the all-black 332nd Fighter Group, which flew as part of the 15th Air Force in the Mediterranean Theater of combat. Parallel to the fighter squadrons, TAAF trained one bomber unit, the 477th FG, flying B-25 medium bombers. The war ended before the bomber unit could be deployed for combat.

Five cadets graduated from the TAAF flight training program on March 6, 1942: Captain Benjamin O. Davis Jr. and lieutenants Lemuel Custis, George S. Roberts, Charles DeBow Jr., and Mac Ross. These survivors of the rigorous program earned their wings and entered the ranks of commissioned officers in the elite Army Air Corps. This small cadre of military aviators became the core element in the newly organized 99th Pursuit Squadron. Just three months had passed since Pearl Harbor and the United States was now at war with the Axis powers in Europe and the Pacific. The lingering question for these black military pilots—and the growing company of black pilots who would soon join them—was whether the Army Air Corps (renamed the Army Air Forces in 1942) would embrace racial equality. Winning their wings at Tuskegee was just a first step, if an historic one, but there would be further trials ahead once they reached the arena of combat.

Benjamin O. Davis Jr. stood out among the newly minted military pilots. The son of an army general, Benjamin O. Davis Sr., then the sole black general in the army, the young Davis brought considerable experience and professionalism to Tuskegee. He was also a graduate of the United States Military Academy at West Point. While at the West Point, he had endured bigotry and racism; from 1932 to 1936, in fact, other cadets shunned him merely because of his race. Being disciplined and committed to a career in the army, Davis held on during those cruel years of isolation and humiliation. In 1936, he applied for acceptance into the Army Air Corps, but was turned down. He then served as a regular army officer prior to his assignment to Tuskegee, where he eventually gained entrance into the flight training program at the TAAF. Upon earning his wings, Davis found himself singled out by Colonel Parrish for appointment as commander of the 99th Pursuit Squadron. Davis was a highly trained professional and disciplined soldier, an officer who quickly won the respect of his peers and Colonel Parrish and his staff of white officers in charge of the advanced phases of flight training.

TOP Major James Ellison, Tuskegee Army Air Field commander, returns Mac Ross's salute as he reviews the first class cadets along the flight line in 1941.

BOTTOM Armorers of the 332nd Fighter Group carry .50 caliber ammunition belts at Selfridge Field, Michigan. The wartime training of ground and support personnel became a vital part of the Tuskegee airmen operations.

Pilots of the 332nd Fighter Group train for overseas deployment at Selfridge Field, Michigan, late in 1943.

In April, 1943, the 99th Fighter Squadron with Davis in command departed on a troop ship from New York City for North Africa. This date marked an important milestone for the TAAF and all who had worked tirelessly to gain acceptance for blacks in military aviation.

Some black aviators, however, trained in the war years in a context of frustration and delay, never seeing active service in a combat zone. This was the melancholy fate of the 477th Bombardment Group. The all-black unit was formally activated on January 15, 1944. It was then assigned for training at the spacious Selfridge Field in Michigan. This posting proved to be short-lived. In May, the group found itself reassigned to the smaller Godman Field in Kentucky. The reasons for the abrupt move related to fears of racial upheaval (Detroit had been the scene of a race riot in 1943). The Army Air Forces had trained the requisite number of black bomber pilots for the 477th, but there remained a severe shortage of navigators and bombardiers. The air unit remained poorly staffed during the final months of the war. In the spring of 1945, when the Army ordered the 477th Bombardment Group to Freeman Field in Indiana, racial tensions flared when members of the air unit protested the segregation of the officers club. The so-called Freeman Field riot showcased

RIGHT Black bomber crew consult a map prior to a training mission.

BELOW A 617th Bombardment Squadron crew chief tests the port engine of a B-25 bomber, ca. 1944.

BOTTOM Aviation cadets at the Tuskegee Army Air Field are reviewed by Major James Ellison and his staff, 1941.

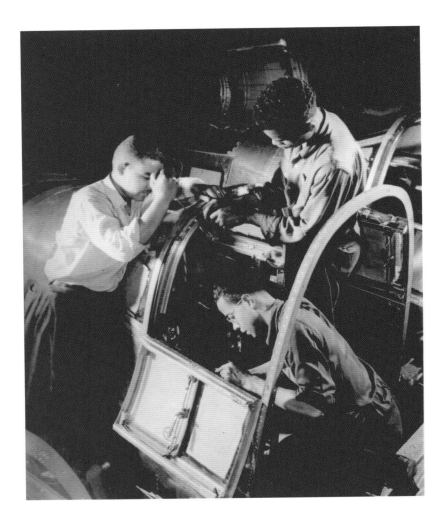

African Americans at home worked in war factories, in this case building the P-51 fighters used by the Tuskegee Airmen.

the inequities and tensions associated with the War Department's effort to maintain a separate black air arm.

There were racial tensions as well in wartime Tuskegee. Agatha Davis reported in one letter to her husband, Colonel Benjamin O. Davis Jr., then serving in Italy with the 332nd Fighter Group, that in the town "tempers were short" and there had been one incident where a man nearly lost his life. The incident arose when a black MP attempted to escort back to the air base two men who were drunk after a "night on the town." A white deputy assaulted the black MP in a violent manner requiring the MP to be hospitalized. She concluded: "things have calmed down but it is a very uneasy peace" (Letter of Agatha Davis, dated May 17, 1944, to Benjamin O. Davis Jr.).

One important stateside initiative to rally blacks for the war effort and foster goodwill among the races was the Double V Campaign. The idea originated with a prominent black newspaper

the *Pittsburgh Courier*. The essential idea was for a "double victory" in the war—a triumph over the Axis powers and a triumph at home to end racial discrimination. The slogan won over patriotic African Americans to affirm their support of the war and also to register their determination to achieve racial justice, seeing the crucible of war as a means to bring about profound change in American social life. The *Pittsburgh Courier* reminded its readers that President Roosevelt had articulated the principle of freedom as a key motive for the Allies to resist Nazi Germany and militarist Japan. The Double V Campaign pushed for freedom at home and abroad.

The Tuskegee experiment's manifest success applied renewed pressure for the abandonment of formal segregation in the armed forces. Running a separate "all-black air force," the army discovered, was costly, grossly inefficient, and increasingly difficult to maintain in the light of sacrifices to the war effort by the African American community.

Tuskegee cadets gather at formal assembly during training in 1942.

LEFT A maintenance crew of the 477th Bombardment Group prepares for a training mission in 1944. The men in this air unit went through extensive training late in World War II. The war ended before they were deployed to a combat front.

BELOW Armament technicians of the 619th Bombardment Squadron mount a .50 caliber machine gun to a B-25 medium bomber.

OPPOSITE PAGE
TOP Lieutenant A. A. Rayner Jr., 616th Bombardment Squadron, and his crew pose in front of their B-25 medium bomber at Godman, Kentucky. *Standing left to right:* Rayner, Samuel R. Hunter, Edward R. Gilson. *Kneeling left to right:* James C. McClain, David L. Glenn, and Samuel L. Davis.

BOTTOM LEFT A 618th Bombardment Squadron armorer loads a practice bomb into the bay of a B-25 bomber.

BOTTOM RIGHT Armament technicians of the 619th Bombardment Squadron load a bomb carrier at Godman Field, Kentucky.

CHAPTER 5

THE TUSKEGEE AIRMEN

THE LONG-AWAITED DAY FINALLY CAME ON APRIL 4, 1943—the 99th Fighter Squadron departed Tuskegee for deployment to the European theater of combat. The passage to the war zone included a long train ride to New York City, where they boarded the ocean liner *Mariposa* bound for Casablanca in Morocco. The arduous period of training had ended. The Tuskegee airmen were going to join the 12th Air Force in the Mediterranean Theater of combat. Once in North Africa, the all-black squadron took a train to Oujda, near Fez, where they underwent briefings and orientation in their new P-40 fighters.

The squadron entered the war with high expectations and great morale. Training for the North African action had been a prolonged

LEFT Bond drive poster from 1944 showing Tuskegee Airman

exercise in hard work and dedication. The whole enterprise began on January 16, 1941 when the 99th was formed at the newly organized Tuskegee Army Air Field. Basic training had opened with just thirteen cadets. Those days of flying PT-17 and AT-6 trainers were now in the distant past. Benjamin O. Davis Jr., now a lieutenant colonel, led the 99th Fighter Squadron. His background as a professional soldier with a West Point education gave his leadership immediate credibility. The 99th also included a pool of skilled ground crew specialists and mechanics. These men had trained in various Air Corps training facilities in the United States, on a segregated basis, and then joined the 99th Fighter Squadron.

INTO COMBAT

By May 1943, the orientation phase ended. The 99th was sent to a frontline assignment in Tunisia. They flew their P-40s to Farjouna, where they joined the 33rd Fighter Group of the 64th Wing of the 12th Air Support Command (later the 12th Tactical Command). They flew their first combat mission against enemy positions on the island of Pantelleria in the Mediterranean Sea on June 6. The pilots on this historic mission included lieutenants William A. Campbell, Charles B. Hall, Clarence Jamison, and James R. Wiley. Later that same month, the 99th acquired additional pilots: Charles Dryden, Willie Ashley, Sidney Brooks, Lee Rayford, Leon Roberts, and Spann Watson. On July 2, the squadron scored its first air victory—on his eighth mission over Pantelleria Charles Hall downed a German Messerschmitt Bf-109. This celebrated victory was unfortunately overshadowed by the death of two pilots in the 99th in air accidents.

By the fall of 1943, the 99th Fighter Squadron had moved to Licata, Sicily, as part of the larger invasion of Italy. In this context, pilots of the 99th flew numerous patrol and strike missions, finding more than one occasion to attack Axis supply lines and communications centers. By September, the 99th had moved to Paestum airfield near Salerno. Lt. Colonel Davis now assumed command of the 332nd Fighter Group (FG), an air unit that included the 99th with the newly minted 100th, 301st, and 302nd fighter squadrons. The three new squadrons greatly enhanced the strength of the Tuskegee airmen in the war zone. The pilots in the 332nd represented a well-trained group with experience flying a variety of combat aircraft, including the P-47, P-40, and P-39 fighters. Once the 332nd FG

TOP LEFT Lt. Colonel Benjamin O. Davis Jr. (*left*) with airman of the 99th Fighter Squadron, North Africa, May 1943.

TOP RIGHT Colonel Davis poses next to his P-40 dubbed Agita Jo.

LEFT Benjamin O. Davis Jr. established a reputation for discipline and professionalism as the commander of the 99th Fighter Squadron.

reached Ramitelli, Italy in 1944, they flew late model P-51 Mustang fighters, then the most advanced fighter interceptor in the Army Air Forces.

In the midst of the Sicilian campaign, the 99th Fighter Squadron faced a serious challenge from within the 12th Air Support Command: Major General Edwin J. House, the commander, submitted a highly negative report on the fighting competence of the all-black squadron. Faced with such internal criticism, Colonel Davis returned to the United States to confront the charges. He realized that such criticism represented a serious threat to the survival of the 99th Fighter Squadron, even the larger Tuskegee "experiment."

While Colonel Davis was in the United States, the war in Italy continued at a fast pace. George "Spanky" Roberts assumed command of the 99th Fighter Squadron. Roberts was a member of the first graduating class at Tuskegee. He enjoyed a positive reputation among the Tuskegee airmen for his great aptitude as a combat pilot and manifest gifts as an air commander. Roberts led the 99th during an active phase of the Italian campaign, being attached to the 79th Fighter Group. In November, the 79th FG moved to Magna Italy, flying a heavy burden of ground attack missions. At the end of that month, the 79th flew a total of twenty-six missions in one day, with the 99th flying a record total of nine missions. Roberts displayed great effectiveness as a leader, winning the respect of the other all-white air units in the 79th Fighter Group.

Prior to January 1944 the 99th scored a single air victory against the Axis air forces. At the end of that month, as the Allies engaged the enemy at the Anzio landings, the 99th entered a highly productive period. Flying P-40s, the Tuskegee airmen downed eight enemy aircraft over the beachhead at Anzio in one day. The score continued to mount: four German aircraft downed on January 28, one on February 5, and three more on February 7. In a two-week period, the 99th had achieved a seven-to-one kill ratio in air combat. The outstanding record caught the attention of Army Air Forces commander Henry "Hap" Arnold, who awarded the 99th an official commen-

ABOVE Black aviator with the 99th Fighter Squadron

LEFT Charles Hall of Brazil, Indiana, downed an FW-190 while on an escort mission on July 21, 1943. This marked the first air victory for the United States by a black airmen in the European Theater.

George S. "Spanky" Roberts earned a reputation for aggressive leadership. He led the 99th in January 1944 during the Anzio campaign. Roberts returned to the United States after completing seventy-eight combat missions.

OPPPOSITE

TOP Benjamin O. Davis Jr. bids farewell to the 99th Fighter Squadron at Licata, Sicily, in August 1943. He returned to the United States for a brief period of time when he defended the operational record of the squadron. He assumed command of the new 332nd fighter Group in 1944.

CENTER LEFT Colonel Davis describes a combat mission where Charles Hall scored the first air victory for the 99th Fighter Squadron, North Africa, 1943.

CENTER RIGHT Major George S. "Spanky" Roberts. He commanded the 99th Fighter Squadron in winter of 1943–1944, and is remembered for his leadership skills and exemplary skills as a fighter pilot.

BOTTOM Airmen of the 332nd Fighter Group study map.

dation for their aggressiveness and skill in battle. For the Tuskegee airmen, the Anzio campaign represented an important milestone—they were no longer apprentice pilots, but seasoned combatants in the air war in Europe.

By 1944, there were dramatic changes in organization and the operational life of the Tuskegee airmen. For months, the black pilots had been assigned tactical missions, flying coastal patrols and assisting Allied ground troops in their advance northward against the German enemy. The Anzio operations signaled a new posture of aggressiveness for the 99th Fighter Squadron. By April, the squadron was reassigned again, this time attached to the 324th Fighter Group. They participated in Operation Strangle, the air campaign to isolate the besieged German defenders in the celebrated battle for Monte Cassino.

On June 6, the day of the Normandy landings, the newly organized 332nd FG found itself attached to the 15th Air Force. As a four squadron fighter group, the 332nd then began the transition to P-51 Mustangs, which were painted with the distinctive RED TAILS livery that became the signature image of the Tuskegee airmen. One notable achievement for the fighter group during this period was the combat sortie of Gwynne Peirson of the 302nd Squadron. Flying a P-51, Peirson sank an enemy destroyer in the Gulf of Venezia. This

ABOVE Benjamin O. Davis Jr., commander of the 99th Fighter Squadron, stands beside his P-40 Fighter Agita Jo. Davis led the 99th in their first combat deployment in North Africa, 1943.

TOP RIGHT Fighter pilot Elwood T. Driver and his armorer inspect a bomb rack on his P-40 prior to a combat mission.

CEBTER RIGHT A P-40 of the 99th Fighter Squadron takes off from Licata, Sicily, in 1943.

BOTTOM RIGHT Members of the 99th Fighter Squadron pose for picture during the Anzio Beachead operation, ca. February 1944.

ABOVE A P-40 fighter is serviced as pilot and ground crew look on, 1943.

LEFT Mechanics service a P-40 fighter aircraft of the 99th Fighter Squadron.

achievement represented the first time a naval vessel was sunk by machine gun fire alone.

On June 7, 1944, Davis and his airmen took up residence at the Ramitelli air base where they would stay until V-E Day. Located in central Italy, near the Adriatic Sea, Ramatelli offered spacious and well-appointed facilities. The runway was constructed with perforated steel mats, then a widely used means to establish improvised and safe airstrips for take-

Writing home was a high priority for all personnel, officers, and enlisted men alike. Here, Herbert Carter of the 99th Fighter Squadron writes a letter while seated on the wing of a P-40 fighter aircraft.

offs and landings. Given its location, Ramatelli was ideally situated for the black airmen to rendezvous quickly with bombers from the 15th Air Force en route to targets in Germany and Central Europe. As the war drew to its finale, the black airmen flew the best fighter aircraft in the inventory of the Army Air Forces, most notably the P-51D Mustang fighters.

Davis—now a full colonel—commanded all operations out of Ramatelli. One of his strict requirements for the pilots related to fighter escort discipline: he insisted that his fighter escorts never leave the bombers, stay close in, and provide proper defense. Davis did not permit his flyers to abandon escort duty for any targets of opportunity. One result of this practice was the high regard B-24 crews had for the black airmen, who routinely offered close support on all missions deep into enemy territory.

Ramatelli—although segregated and isolated—soon boasted many amenities. There were clubs for both the officers and enlisted men. There were drinks, music, and time to swim in the warm waters of the nearby Adriatic. The home of the 332nd also became the destination for black entertainers and celebrities. Heavyweight boxing champion Joe Louis, himself a sergeant in the U.S. Army, made a courtesy call at the all-black air base. There were movies and USO shows to round out the social life at Ramatelli. At the height of the war, life in 332nd allowed for pleasant pursuits such as lavish Thanksgiving and Christmas dinners, gift packages from home, furloughs to Naples and other Italian cities, and sports competition in the 15th Air Force. Morale remained high, a contrast to the early years in North Africa.

OPPOSITE
TOP A 99th Fighter Squadron pilot studies a map prior to a mission, 1943.

BOTTOM A Red Tail P-51 Mustang lands at Ramatelli, Italy, on the segmented metal runway.

ABOVE Benjamin O. Davis Jr. stands next to a P-47 fighter aircraft, which was flown briefly by pilots of the 332nd Fighter Group in 1944.

TOP LEFT Tuskegee airman Edward C. Gleed of Lawrence, Kansas, at Ramatelli, Italy, in March 1945.

CENTER LEFT Colonel Benjamin O. Davis Jr, commander of the 332nd Fighter Group with Edward C. Gleed at Ramatelli, Italy, in March 1945.

BOTTOM LEFT Tuskegee airmen depart parachute shack at Ramatelli, Italy, in March 1945.

PILOT-Capt. A. D. Turner.
C/CHIEF-S/Sgt. ?. Cochran.
Asst- Sgt. C. ? antley.
C/ARM- Col. H. Beguesse.

ABOVE Lieutenant Andrew D. Turner prepares for combat mission at Ramatelli, Italy. Turner completed sixty-nine combat missions and was awarded the Distinguished Flying Cross.

RIGHT Lieutenants Andrew D. Turner and Clarence D. Lester discuss air combat mission after their safe return to Ramatelli, 1944.

Black airmen gather for a drink and conversation at their rest camp in Naples, Italy. *Left to right:* Lieutenant Wylie Selden, Captain Fred Hutchinson, unidentified Red Cross worker, Lieutenants George Gray and F. Johnson.

OPPOSITE Tuskegee airmen adjust survival gear. *Left to right:* William Campbell and Thurston L Gaines.

The flight surgeon for the Ramatelli air base was the talented Major Vance H. Marchbanks Jr. The son of an army cavalry officer, Marchbanks had graduated from Howard University before he entered the army in 1941. Specializing in aviation medicine, he joined the 332nd in 1944, at the time of the air unit's deployment to the Italian campaign. Despite shortages and a paucity of trained personnel, Marchbanks administered the medical program at Ramatelli with great efficiency and professionalism.

As a vital part of the 15th Air Force, the 332nd FG began bomber escort duty in July 1944. Colonel Davis had returned to the war zone and, commanding the 332nd FG, led the first bomber escort mission. Pilots of the 332nd made their rendezvous with B-24 bombers of the 15th Air Force and flew escort to Munich Germany in P-47s. In one encounter with the Luftwaffe, eight P-47s attacked eighteen enemy fighters, downing five and damaging one.

The month of July saw some dramatic air victories. On July 12, Joseph Elsberry downed three German Fw-190 fighters on an escort mission to Friederichshafen, Germany. Three B-24s were lost to enemy flak batteries. Always attentive to their charges, the escorting black pilots kept close to two crippled B-24s as they made their way home.

Airmen of the 332nd Fighter Group attend briefing prior to mission. *Left to right:* Robert W. Williams, William H. Holloman, Ronald W. Reeves, and Walter W. Downs.

ABOVE Commander of the 332nd Fighter Group Benjamin O. Davis Jr. briefs pilots prior to combat mission, Ramatelli, Italy, 1944.

TOP LEFT Control tower at Ramatelli air base, Italy in 1944.

CENTER LEFT John T. Fields, an armament specialist in the 332nd, loads a P-51 Mustang with .50 caliber ammunition.

BOTTOM LEFT A P-51 Mustang of the 332nd Fighter Group, Ramatelli, 1944.

STRATEGIC BOMBING CAMPAIGN

Bombing missions by the 15th Air Force deep into German-controlled territory meant flying over the Alps, which was always a perilous journey. Enemy anti-aircraft batteries were well-positioned near all strategic targets—factories, marshalling yards, and airfields. Flying in close formation for defensive protection, the lumbering B-24s found themselves in the crosshairs of enemy flak batteries. Victims of such withering fire were chosen in an arbitrary way, a sudden explosion reducing a bomber to a ball of fire. Some aircraft fell from the sky in flames, while others just fell out of formation and crashed. Enemy fire did its job in unpredictable ways—killing the cockpit crew, damaging engines, igniting a fire in the fuselage, or causing the wings to collapse. Once an aircraft was stricken, there were anxious moments before the crew or some of the crew managed to parachute to safety. If German interceptors reached the bomber formation, as Luftwaffe commander Adolf Galland once remarked, it was easy to hit a target, given their tight formations. A straggler was always vulnerable to enemy fighters, and, accordingly, such damaged aircraft became an object of concern for Tuskegee airmen who flew escort.

The attrition in American bombers—deployed for mostly daytime missions—remained high throughout the war. The repeated

Benjamin O. Davis Jr. (*center*) escorts General Ira Eaker, a high-ranking Army Air Forces commander, on a tour of the Ramatelli air base in 1944.

bomber sorties against the Ploesti oil fields in 1944, as one example, was costly in the extreme—the United States lost 286 heavy bombers and 2,829 men were killed or captured. The 332nd participated in the high-risk Ploesti raids, but strangely did not lose one escort fighter to the enemy. However, James Walker, who was shot down over Yugoslavia on July 22, but parachuted to safety. Later he was picked up by partisans and joined nine other downed American airmen in German-occupied Yugoslavia. After crossing three hundred miles over mountainous terrain, Walker made it back to his base. Andrew D. Marshall faced a similar struggle for survival in Greece when anti-aircraft fire severely damaged his fighter, forcing him to parachute to safety. He narrowly escaped from his burning aircraft. Once on the ground, Marshall managed to elude the enemy until Greek partisans rescued him.

In the summer of 1944, 332nd pilots shot down two Macchi fighters of Benito Mussolini's rump state in Northern Italy. While this victory and others were celebrated as important benchmarks in the Italian air campaign, there were constant reminders of the perils

Lt. Andrew D. Marshall was downed by enemy flak in a mission over Greece in the autumn of 1944. Greek partisans hid him from the German occupying army. Here, Marshall tells of his harrowing experience and rescue to an officer of the 51st Troop Carrier Wing.

LEFT Two of the 332nd Fighter Group's most talented combat pilots, Clarence D. Lester and Wendell O. Pruitt, shake hands in front of a P-51 Mustang.

BOTTOM Ground crew of the 332nd Fighter Group mount drop tank on P-51 Mustang fighter aircraft. External fuel tanks allowed fighter aircraft to make long-distance escort missions into Nazi-occupied Europe.

OPPOSITE
TOP Colonel Benjamin O. Davis Jr. sits in cockpit of his P-51 fighter and confers with staff officers: *Left to right:* unknown officer and William R. Thompson, armorer.

BOTTOM Captain Erwin B. Lawrence of Cleveland, Ohio, lost his life while on a strafing mission against a German air base in Greece.

To Bill from his
old buddy. We've
had some swell
together
B. Lawrence

HOW CLARENCE "LUCKY" LESTER EARNED HIS THREE VICTORIES

Lieutenant Clarence D. "Lucky" Lester flew his P-51 Mustang "Miss Pelt" to a remarkable three-victory day on July 18, 1944. Lester won the Distinguished Flying Cross and went on to fly in the postwar integrated U.S. Air Force.

"It was a clear day in July 1944 when the P-51 Mustangs of the 332nd Fighter Group took off from their airfield at Ramitelli, Italy. Our mission was to rendezvous over northern Italy's Po Valley at 25,000 feet with B-17 Flying Fortresses en route to bomb a German airfield in southern Germany. We had been given the task of escorting the bombers to the target and back, providing protection from enemy aircraft. We relished the assignment since it allowed us to conduct a fighter sweep, which meant we provided general cover, but had no specific group of 'Forts' to protect; I flew with the 100th Fighter Squadron. The name 'Lucky' stuck because of all the tight situations from which I had escaped without a scratch or even a bullethole in my aircraft.

"The rendezvous was made on time at 25,000 feet. The bombers always came in higher than planned and continued to climb so that they reached the target well over 30,000 feet (the higher, the safer from ground fire). The other squadrons of the 332nd began their close cover at 27,000 feet. We were around 29,000 feet when bogeys (enemy aircraft) were spotted above us.

"Two Down, One to Go," a painting by William S. Phillips

"We were flying a loose combat formation, 200 feet apart and zig-zagging. The flight leader commanded 'hard right turn and punch tanks' (drop external fuel tanks) when Number Four called that he could not get one of his two tanks off. He was never seen again. At this time, I saw a formation of Messerschmitt Bf-109s straight ahead, but slightly lower; I closed to about 200 feet and started to fire. Smoke began to pour out of the 109 and the aircraft exploded. I was going so fast I was sure I would hit some of the debris from the explosion, but luckily I didn't.

"As I was dodging pieces of aircraft, I saw another 109 to my right, all alone on a heading 90 degrees to mine, but at the same altitude. I turned onto his tail and closed to about 200 feet while firing. His aircraft started to smoke and almost stopped. My closure was so fast I began to overtake him. When I overran him, I looked down to see the enemy pilot emerge from his burning aircraft. I remember seeing his blonde hair as he bailed out at approximately 8,000 feet.

"By this time, I was alone and looking for my flight mates when I spotted the third 109 flying very low, about 1,000 feet off the ground. I dove to the right behind him and opened fire. As I scored hits, he apparently thought he had enough altitude to use a 'split–S' maneuver to evade me (A 'split-S' is a one-half loop going down; the aircraft is rolled upside down and pulled straight through until it is right side up—not recommended below 3,500 feet).

"We were approximately 1,000 feet above the ground and, as I did a diving turn, I saw the 109 go straight into the ground. During the return flight, it took a while to realize how much had happened in that brief span of time (4 to 6 minutes maximum). Everything went the same as in training except for the real bullets. *Real Bullets!!!* Until then the danger of this mission had never occurred to me."

— Clarence D. Lester

ABOVE A group of 332nd fighter pilots assemble next to the P-51 Fighter Skipper's Darling at Ramatelli, Italy.

LEFT Wendell Pruitt chats with his crew chief.

Lieutenant Lee A. Archer, a native of New York City, became one of the most proficient pilots in the 332nd, being highly regarded for his skill, aggressiveness, and gallantry in air combat.

of air combat. Returning pilots reported narrow escapes. The aircraft of the 332nd FG often bore the scars of combat with bullet holes and flak damage to the wings, fuselage, and control surfaces. Others were shot down, captured, and forced to spend the remainder of the war in POW camps. Some Tuskegee airmen were killed in action and their deaths served to mark the tragic course of the war. One example of an untimely and grieved loss was the death of Erwin B. Lawrence of Cleveland, Ohio, who was killed while strafing the Athens Tatoi airfield. The enemy had placed a trip wire to force Lawrence's P-51 into a crash at low altitude, the same hidden or invisible danger that later took the life Kenneth Williams. Captain Lawrence had been part of the original 99th Fighter Squadron.

Clarence "Lucky" Lester made his debut as one of the 332nd FG on July 18, downing a German aircraft (this was later designated as a shared victory). Lester earned additional fame in October 1944, when he shot down three German fighters in one day, one of the more impressive outings for the Tuskegee airmen flying out of Ramatelli.

That summer and fall of 1944, the 332nd engaged in a series of diverse missions against the Axis powers. In July, there was a high-risk mission to the German-controlled Ploesti oil refineries in

Members of the 332nd Fighter Group gather for a briefing.

ABOVE Lieutenant Edward Thomas prepares to depart for a mission in 1944. Thomas survived the war but was killed in an aircraft accident at Tuskegee Army Air Field in 1946.

LEFT Pilots of the 332nd Fighter Group relax at the Three Minute Club at Ramitelli air base, Italy.

OPPOSITE

TOP General Benjamin O. Davis Sr., then the only black general in the U.S. Army, pins a Distinguished Flying Cross on his son, Benjamin O. Davis Jr. in Italy on May 29, 1944.

BOTTOM Lieutenant Wendell O. Pruitt (*right*) greets John F. Briggs. Pruitt won the Distinguished Flying Cross for gallantry in the strafing enemy shipping in June 1944.

ABOVE Captain A. G. McDaniel inspects the damage to his P-51 Mustang after returning from a combat mission over the Danube River. He was hit by a barrage of enemy fire. *Left to right:* Sergeant Richard Adams, Captain McDaniel, Lieutenant James McFatridge, and Ulysses Taylor.

BELOW A ground crewman prepares to close cockpit canopy as pilot William T. Mattison makes last minute checks prior to a combat mission.

Romania, then a fiercely defended fuel source for the entire German military. Repeated raids by the 15th Air Force on Ploesti had led to significant casualties. In August, the 332nd flew repeated sorties as escorts for bombing raids to support the invasion of southern France. There was even an escort mission to Czechoslovakia, a distant target in Central Europe. Luke Weathers and two other Tuskegee airmen escorted a crippled B-24 bomber to safety in England. Weathers was credited with downing two German Bf-109 fighters. With the accumulating victories there were grievous losses; in October alone, the 332nd lost a total of fifteen airmen in air combat.

In a notable October mission, seventy-two aircraft from the 332nd flew north for strafing attacks along the Danube River from Budapest, Hungary, to Bratislava, Czechoslovakia. With heavy cloud cover, only thirty aircraft managed to reach the target area, in this case strafing three enemy airfields along the Danube. The next day, the offensive was renewed, this time with greater numbers and in better weather conditions. During the action Wendell Pruitt set off to down an enemy bomber, only to be attacked suddenly by seven Messerschmitt Bf-109 fighters. Lee Archer, the high-scoring fighter pilot for the Tuskegee airmen, joined in the intense air action. Pruitt downed one enemy bomber and one fighter until his guns jammed. Archer exited from the air combat with no fewer than three downed Bf-109s. Six other Tuskegee airmen scored a single air victory, allowing the 332nd to return home with a total of nine kills for the day.

Flying fighter escort for the 15th Air Force became the singular task for the 332nd in 1945, even as the Allies pushed ahead on two fronts to conquer Nazi Germany. In January, in the depths of a cold winter, the 332nd found itself limited to a mere eleven missions. In February, the tempo increased dramatically with a total of thirty-nine missions.

BELOW Lieutenant Elwood T. Driver jokes for the camera in Licata, Sicily. Driver flew with the 99th Fighter Squadron and would score his first air victory over Anzio in 1944.

Officers of the 332nd Fighter Group. *Bottom row, left to right:* Edward C. Gleed, Nelson Brooks, Benjamin O. Davis Jr., commander, unidentified officer, George S. Roberts, Thomas J. Money. *Top, left to right:* Denzel Harvey, Cyrus W. Perry, Ray B. Ware.

ABOVE Benjamin O. Davis Jr. acknowledges an important milestone—the 200th combat mission of the Tuskegee airmen.

RIGHT Edward M. Thomas at Ramatelli, Italy, in March 1945

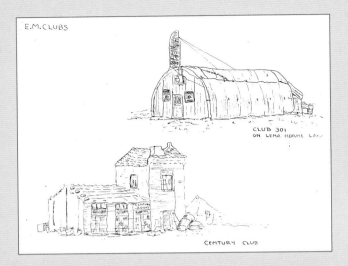

E.M.CLUBS

CLUB 301
ON LENA HORNE LA.

CENTURY CLUB

Series of five sketches of Ramatelli air base from Davis Collection, National Air and Space Museum

E.M.CLUBS

THE HELLION'S DEN
302 EM'S CLUB.

THE CLUB EXOTIC

332 GROUP and HEADQUARTERS
CHAPEL plus MAPHER THEATER

PEASANT'S TRANSPORTATION

IN NEARBY FIELDS

MOUTAS LATRINE
"FLOP HOUSE"

GROUP OPERATIONS
"THE LAST MILE"

FOTO LAB

PARACHUTE SHOW
BRING IT BACK IF IT DOES

RATION AND SALVAGE DUMP

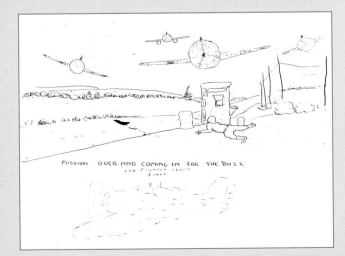

MISSION OVER AND COMING IN FOR THE BUZZ
332 FIGHTER GROUP
ITALY

As the winter months waned, the all-black fighter group found it-self in a series of critical escort missions against key enemy targets. On March 24, Davis led Red Tail escorts to support a 15th Air Force mission to attack the Daimler-Benz factory in Berlin. This particular outing became a daunting one, consisting of a 1,600-mile roundtrip mission. The Luftwaffe—even at this late stage of the war—offered spirited resistance, along with highly effective anti-aircraft batteries. German air defense also included the introduction of a new weapon: the Messerschmitt Me-262 jet fighter. The advanced German jet fighter demonstrated a new level of performance, being capable of speeds 100 mph faster than Allied fighters. The black airmen per-formed in an exemplary fashion on the raid on the Daimler-Benz facility. They faced a group of enemy interceptors that included the Fw-190 and the newly deployed Me-262s. Roscoe C. Brown, Charles Brantly, and Earl Lane each downed one Me-262 jet (prior to this time Allied pilots had downed only two jets). As a consequence of this mission the 332nd received a Distinguished Unit Citation.

April 1 became a momentous day for the 332nd, just as the war was drawing to a close. Tuskegee airmen provided escort for the 47th Bomber Wing in a mission to bomb the railroad marshalling yards in Polten, Austria. When they were returning home, the black pi-lots spotted four enemy FW-190s fighters below the bomber forma-tion. They dove on the enemy aircraft only to realize that they had been drawn into a trap. Suddenly other Luftwaffe aircraft appeared and pressed an attack on the unwary Americans. In the dogfight that followed no fewer than twelve enemy fighters were shot down and three Red Tails were lost. The melee demonstrated the skill of the 332nd in air combat.

That same month the war in Europe was drawing to a close. The 332nd FG, in fact, scored the last four enemy aircraft in the Mediterranean Theater of combat. The tally for the war had been an impressive one: 111 enemy aircraft downed in air combat, and an-other 150 on the ground. The 332nd had lost a total of 66 pilots for all causes, in the States and in the war zone. Some thirty-two black airmen had been shot down and captured.

Ensign Jesse L. Brown looks out from the cockpit of his Grumman F8F Bearcat fighter.
Brown was a pioneering black aviator who died tragically in combat during the Korean War.

CHAPTER 6

AT FULL STRIDE

THE DECADES AFTER WORLD WAR II WERE CHAR-
acterized as an era of significant advances in civil rights. The war
had eroded the older pattern of official racial barriers in military
aviation. Civilian flying, though not strictly defined by policies of
discrimination, was nevertheless a domain where blacks had made
a few inroads. Commercial aviation remained an all-white sphere.
The Tuskegee airmen had demonstrated the capabilities of African
Americans in all phases of flying, shattering the myth that a minor-
ity in American society lacked the aptitude and will to fly advanced
aircraft. The demand for blacks to participate fully in aeronautics
had gained momentum. These same years saw the growing power
of the civil rights movement, which began to challenge entrenched

racial discrimination in education, public accommodations, entertainment, sports, and other professions. Changes in aviation ran parallel to these historic transformations.

A MAJOR HURDLE

The war ended for the Tuskegee airmen in May 1945 with the collapse of Nazi Germany. The many months of active duty flying escort for bombers of the 15th Air Force came to an end. There was a deep sense of satisfaction among the black airmen—pilots and ground crews alike—on the stellar work of the 332nd Fighter Group. As an air unit, the 332nd had performed on par with other fighter groups, shattering the prewar myth that African Americans lacked the aptitude to fly and the requisite aggressiveness of military pilots. They had flown in segregated circumstances, often at odds with the Army Air Forces establishment, and they had scored a decisive victory for racial progress. Simply put, the so-called Tuskegee experiment had worked in a dramatic fashion.

On June 8, 1945, Colonel Benjamin O. Davis Jr. received the coveted Silver Star, a meaningful and deserved recognition of the excellence of his leadership during the final weeks of the war. Shortly after the award ceremony, Colonel Davis and his company of forty officers from the 332nd FG boarded B-17s for the long flight home. His new assignment was the command of the 477th Composite Group, an all-black air unit. The war in the Pacific still raged with all its fury, and there were some rumors afloat that the black pilots, including the bomber crews trained stateside in B-25 medium bombers, would soon be transferred to Asia to join the final assault on Japan. This event never occurred since August 15, 1945 marked V-J Day—the sudden cessation of war in the aftermath of the atomic bombing of Hiroshima and Nagasaki. The 477th Composite Group was assigned to Godman Army Air Field in Kentucky. The air unit consisted of the 99th and the 100th fighter squadrons and 617th and 618th bombardment squadrons. In the immediate postwar years, Davis and his airmen faced the challenge of pursuing their military careers in a still segregated air force. In 1947, the independent air branch of the armed forces, the U.S. Air Force, was created. Initially, the Air Force—following existing military practice—remained segregated.

In early 1946, the old Tuskegee Army Air Field closed as part of the postwar drawdown; officers were then reassigned to Godman.

Ground crew of the 618th Bombardment Group prepare a B-25 bomber for takeoff, September 1944.

Nearly one thousand men had earned their wings at Tuskegee. Throughout these war years, Noel Parrish oversaw the flight instruction for the black pilots, and, in many ways, he was an indispensable figure in making the Tuskegee flight program such a success. Parrish later advanced to the rank of general in the Air Force, wrote about the problems of segregation in the armed forces, and worked tirelessly to bring about racial integration in the armed forces. His 1947 paper entitled "The Segregation of Negroes in the Army Air Forces" for the Air Command and Staff School of the Air University did much to clarify the issues and make the case for integration. Parrish not only pointed to the moral questions raised by continued racial segregation in the armed forces, but also argued that the entire enterprise was inefficient and costly to maintain. Inevitably, the Parrish's position prevailed; in July 1948, President Harry S. Truman issued Executive Order 9981, calling for an end to segregation in the military. Coincidental to Truman's executive order was the creation of the President's Committee on Equality of Treatment and Opportunity in the Armed Forces. This oversight group later became

known as the Fahy Committee, under the chairmanship of Charles Fahy. The biracial committee included, among its various public figures, James V. Forrestal, Secretary of Defense, along with the secretaries of the army, navy, and Air Force. One of the mandates of the Fahy Committee was to carry out provisions of Truman's Executive Order 9981.

Even before Colonel Davis returned from the war, the tensions associated with racial discrimination in the Army Air Forces had surfaced in a dramatic way—the Freeman Field Mutiny. In April 1945, just as the war in Europe was drawing to a close and the 332nd was flying its last escort missions, the 477th Bombardment Group found itself embroiled in a dispute over the segregation of base facilities. The dispute centered on the exclusion of black officers from the Officer's Club at Freeman Field. This decision by white officers in charge at Freeman prompted anger and discontent among the black airmen. Some black officers refused to accept the racial ban, which, in turn, brought threats of reprisal. In time, the black-owned *Pittsburgh Courier* began to report the unrest at Freeman.

The crisis escalated on April 5 when some one hundred black airmen arrived at Freeman for training; this group, it was rumored, would descend on the all-white officer's club to force the issue. That evening, in fact, four black airmen did attempt to enter the segregated club only to be turned away. A half hour later, another nineteen black officers were turned back at the entrance to the officer's club. The names of all nineteen black officers were taken. They were then summarily arrested and confined to their quarters. Several attempts to enter were made that evening with the same result. A total of sixty-one men were arrested. All the arrested officers were released eventually, except the three men who made physical attempts to enter the facility. The incident soon aroused great notoriety and embarrassment for the army. The McCloy Special Troop Policies Committee, set up in 1942, became involved in the Freeman crisis, but did not act decisively, even endorsing the idea that segregation could continue at Freeman. The McCloy committee had emerged in the war under the leadership of John McCloy, the assistant secretary of war, dealing with issues related to black servicemen. Truman Gibson, a prominent black leader and adviser to the War Department, criticized the committee and the army for failure to end racial discrimination. With growing pressure from Congress and civil rights organizations, all charges of mutiny were finally dropped. The arrested black officers were then released without penalty or the

TOP Colonel Benjamin O. Davis Jr. (*far left*) assumed the postwar command of the 477th Composite Group, ca 1946. Davis became the first black officer to command a military base in the United States.

BOTTOM The Fahy Committee on Equality of Treatment in the Armed Forces was an offshoot of President Harry S. Truman's Executive Order 9981, which mandated an end to segregation in the U.S. military. The Fahy Committee is shown here in 1949, meeting with President Truman.

Spann Watson flew with the Tuskegee airmen in World War II and in the post war period continued his flying career. His career overlapped with the creation of the United States Air Force as an independent branch of the armed forces.

ordeal of a courtmartial. The appointment of Colonel Davis as commander of the 477th offered a new context for the air unit to resume its activities. However, the Freeman Field dispute added additional weight to the growing campaign to integrate the armed services. For Tuskegee airmen returning from the war, the Freeman incident led to frustration and bitterness—and a reminder that racial discrimination at home remained a serious and chronic problem.

Life for black airmen in the postwar years remained active, even as the independent Air Force began to take shape and racial integration became the established practice. Initially, the 477th Composite Group flew World War II aircraft, the fighter squadrons employing P-47s and the bomber squadrons the venerable B-25 medium bombers. The air group performed well, passing the operational readiness inspections effortlessly and winning the coveted Air Force gunnery

TOP A maintenance crew of the 477th Composite Group prepare an engine for an overhaul.

LEFT Lieutenant Floyd Thompson, 332nd Fighter Wing, in the cockpit of his Republic P-47N Thunderbolt fighter aircraft.

ABOVE RIGHT Republic P-47N Thunderbolts of the all-black 332nd Fighter Wing at Lockbourne Air Force Base in Ohio.

ABOVE Airmen of the 477th Composite Group in front of a B-25 bomber

LEFT Benjamin O. Davis Jr. assumed command of Lockbourne Air Force Base (Ohio) as a major postwar assignment. He is shown here greeting General Elwood Quesada at Lockbourne in 1946.

OPPOSITE Lieutenant William E. "Earl" Brown Jr. is seen here alongside his North American F-86 Sabre jet fighter in Korea, 1953. He had flown a total of 125 combat missions in the Korean War.

competition in 1949. The postwar years saw the gradual transition to jet aircraft; some veteran Tuskegee airmen who remained in the military also made the shift. By the time of the Korean War (1950–1953), formal or institutionalized segregation had ended, although racial discrimination persisted in the military as it did in society at large.

William E. Brown Jr. was a black aviator who flew with the U.S. Air Force in the Korean War. Later rising in the ranks to major general, Brown flew F-86 Sabres in the Korean conflict, completing some 125 combat missions. As a career officer, Brown later flew another one hundred missions in the Vietnam War. Clarence "Lucky" Lester, the veteran fighter pilot with the 332nd Fighter Group, continued as a military pilot with the Air Force in the postwar years, flying late-model jets and serving in West Germany.

Ensign Jesse L. Brown became the first black pilot in the U.S. Navy. He had enlisted in the Navy Reserve in 1946 when he was nineteen years old. Later, he qualified for training as a naval aviator at Pensacola, Florida, and was the sole black cadet. He earned his wings at the age of twenty-two. In the Korean War, Jesse Brown served with a squadron stationed on the U.S.S. Leyte, flying F4U Corsairs. In the difficult early days of the war, Brown flew strafing missions in support of the UN troops retreating from the invading North Korean communist forces. On December 4, 1950, he crashed behind enemy lines after a withering round of anti-aircraft fire. Fellow naval aviator Tom Hudner then made a difficult landing near the crash site in hopes of rescuing Brown. In near-zero weather, Hudner climbed up a snow-covered hillside to reach his downed squadron mate. Upon reaching the smoking wreckage, Hudner discovered that Brown was badly injured, barely conscious, and in need of immediate medical attention. When a rescue helicopter arrived, a desperate effort ensued to save Brown's life. The extraordinary steps taken proved unsuccessful. Ensign Brown died, but before he lost consciousness he gave Hudner a message to deliver to his wife. In the aftermath of this incident, Ensign Brown was awarded posthumously the Distinguished Flying Cross. For his initiative and bravery, Hudner received a Congressional Medal of Honor. In 1972, the U.S. Navy named a frigate the U.S.S. Jesse L. Brown.

Another pioneer military aviator during the Korean War was Frank E. Peterson Jr. His decision to become a Marine aviator set the stage for an impressive career in the U.S. military. He flew combat missions in both the Korean and Vietnam wars, becoming the

first black pilot to command a squadron in either the Marines or U.S. Navy. He later advanced to the rank of lieutenant general in the Marines. There were other breakthroughs that marked the progress of African Americans in military aviation: Lloyd Newton and Joseph N. "Pete" Peterson both qualified for the elite Air Force demonstration team, the Thunderbirds. With time, African Americans, especially in the military, placed less and less stress on firsts as a signal of their growing acceptance in the ranks of military aviation.

During the postwar years, Benjamin O. Davis Jr. emerged as the most senior African American officer in the U.S. Air Force. Between 1946 and 1949 Davis commanded the 332nd Fighter Wing at Lockbourne Air Base, near Columbus, Ohio, where as base commander he oversaw the work of a mixed group of black and white personnel. His inspired leadership set an important precedent for all black officers who followed. Still a colonel, he led the 51st Fighter Interceptor Wing in Korea and was later director of operations and

Frank E. Peterson served as a combat pilot in both the Korean and Vietnam wars. A Marine Corps officer, he later advanced to the rank of lieutenant general.

An integrated Air Force flight crew in the Korean War with their B-26 Invader aircraft. *Left to right*: Dennis Judd, Donald Mansfield, and Bill Ralston.

training for the Far East Air Force in Japan. He was promoted to brigadier general in 1954. His rise in the ranks was steady and linked to key assignments, serving as the commander of the 13th Air Force at Clark Air Base in the Philippines, among other posts. Davis ended his impressive years in the military as a lieutenant general in the U.S. Air Force. In 1998, he was awarded his fourth star, as a gesture of appreciation for his stellar career.

Daniel "Chappie" James emerged in the postwar years as a dynamic leader of a new generation of black military pilots. Trained at Tuskegee, he was a flight leader for a fighter squadron at Clark Field in the Philippines in the late 1940s. With the Korean War, he flew 101 combat sorties in P-51 Mustangs and F-80 jets. His career took a sharp upward trajectory in the 1950s, first at Otis Air Force Base between 1953 and 1956, where he attained the rank of major. A short stint at the Air Command and Staff School in 1957 marked him for a leadership role in the Pentagon. For two years, 1960 to

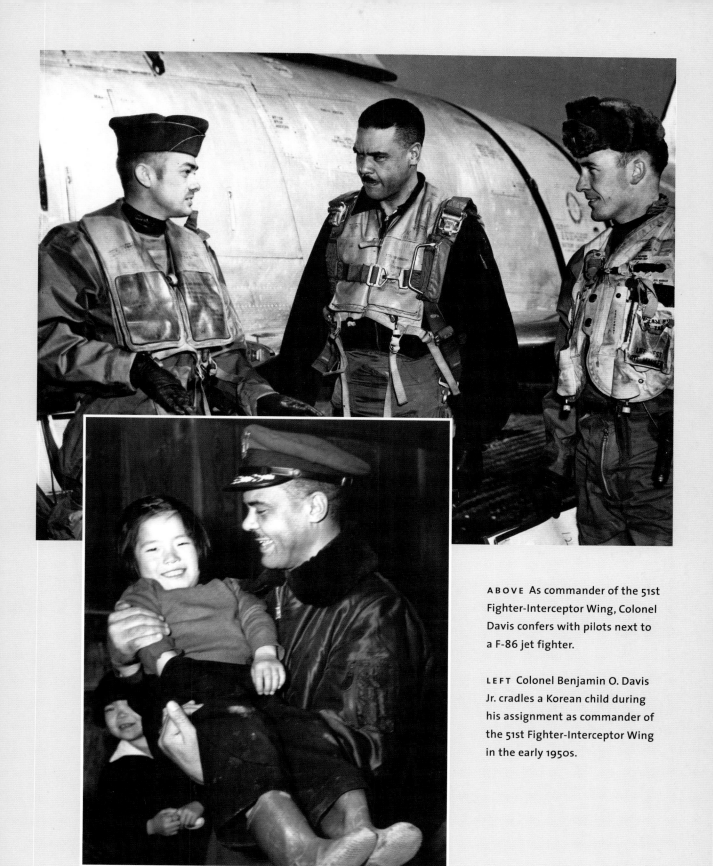

ABOVE As commander of the 51st Fighter-Interceptor Wing, Colonel Davis confers with pilots next to a F-86 jet fighter.

LEFT Colonel Benjamin O. Davis Jr. cradles a Korean child during his assignment as commander of the 51st Fighter-Interceptor Wing in the early 1950s.

ABOVE General Daniel "Chappie" James in 1975, shortly after he had assumed command of the North American Air Defense Command (NORAD) and awarded his fourth star.

TOP RIGHT Brigadier General Benjamin O. Davis Jr. greets Chiang Kai-shek, the leader of the Nationalist Chinese. In the mid-1950s, Davis served as the vice commander of the 13th Air Force stationed on Taiwan.

BOTTOM RIGHT James poses in front of his McDonnell-Douglas F-4C Phantom in Thailand during the Vietnam War. While attached to the 8th Tactical Wing, he flew 78 combat missions.

OPPOSITE Captain Joseph N. "Pete" Peterson flew with the U.S. Air Force Thunderbirds, an aerial demonstration team, in the early 1980s. Peterson was killed tragically on January 12, 1982 while performing a loop with fellow pilots in a practice session.

ABOVE Colonel Fred V. Cherry, an Air Force pilot, endured seven years as a prisoner of war in North Vietnam. He is shown here at his release at Clark air base in the Philippines where he is greeted by Lieutenant Colonel James Warren.

RIGHT In 1974, Captain Lloyd Newton became the first black pilot selected for the elite Air Force demonstration team, the Thunderbirds.

1964, James served in England. With the Vietnam War, he found himself reassigned to a combat zone: he would fly seventy-eight combat missions. Now a colonel, he assumed the position of vice commander of the 33rd Tactical Fighter Wing at Elgin Air Force base. After the assignment in the late 1960s, James was promoted to brigadier general in the U.S. Air Force, taking command of Wheelus Air Force base in Libya. Other prestigious and significant postings followed, including deputy assistant secretary of defense for public affairs and vice commander of the Military Airlift Command at Scott Air Force Base in Illinois.

In 1975, James became the first African American to attain four stars or the rank of full general. Coincidental to this singular achievement, James took command of the North American Air Defense Command (NORAD). His career had been a varied one from Tuskegee, to frontline combat air sorties in Korea and Vietnam, to leadership positions in the Pentagon. Throughout his career James had taken a keen interest in recruiting talented black youth for military aviation. His life ended in an untimely way in 1978, in retirement, the victim of sudden heart attack.

The U.S. Air Force Thunderbirds

John W. Greene enters cockpit of his Kinner Sportster. Greene's flying career covered several decades. On the eve of World War II, he was one three black pilots who had earned a transport pilot's license. He emerged as a prominent figure in general aviation and an educator.

RACIAL EQUALITY IN CIVILIAN FLYING

World War II came to an end in the summer of 1945, signaling vast changes in American life—and for some African Americans the context offered an opportunity to renew their struggle to gain racial equality in all phases of civilian flying. Some of the veterans from the pioneering years of the 1930s had passed away, most notably William J. Powell Jr. who died in 1943. A great visionary, Powell would be missed and his flying club in Los Angeles never regained its former dynamism. In Chicago, Cornelius Coffey persisted as a prominent figure in general aviation in the postwar years. His Coffey School of Aeronautics had graduated no fewer than 1,500 students between 1938 and 1945. During peacetime, Coffey maintained an active role as a flight instructor in Chicago. Others from

John Greene stands next to an Aeronca 7AC Champion at the Columbia Air Center on Croom, Maryland.

John Greene was not only a talented pilot, but also a keen advocate of promoting aviation within the African American community. He is shown here (*seated, center*) discussing model building by black youth.

the old Chicago circle went their own way. The flamboyant John C. Robinson eventually returned to Ethiopia to resume his flying career. He died in 1954 in a plane crash while making an emergency delivery of medical supplies. Other African American fliers—Willa Brown, Chauncey Spencer, and C. Alfred Anderson—remained in aviation during the postwar years, but not as active leaders.

During the postwar years, John W. Greene joined Coffey as a leading figure in general aviation. A contemporary of both Coffey and Powell, Greene earned his pilot's license in 1929, which, for the time, was a significant personal achievement. Early on, Greene displayed an aptitude for sport flying and aircraft design and had a keen interest in teaching black youth the fundamentals of flight. Greene taught an aviation mechanics course at the Phelps Vocational School in Washington, D.C. At nearby Groom, Maryland, Greene worked with others to set up a small aviation school. The enterprising Greene demonstrated a flair for both flying and aeronautical education.

The postwar years also became the context for some talented black aviators to design their own experimental aircraft. One of the most remarkable fliers was Neil Loving from Detroit. As an eleven-year-old, Loving had been inspired by Charles Lindbergh's 1927 transatlantic flight. In the midst of the Great Depression, the determined young Loving enrolled in Detroit's Cass Technical High School intent on a career in aviation. By 1939, he had soloed. His interest in aircraft design led him to build gliders, and his first successful design, the S-2, flying in 1941. Later, during the war, Loving crashed his S-2 and was seriously injured. Doctors had to amputate both his legs. After a long period of hospitalization and recovery, the determined Loving returned to flying. By 1946, fitted with wood, legs, he was airborne again. He opened the Wayne School of Aeronautics and began to design his own airplane. His experimental aircraft, the WR-1 (dubbed Loving's Love) was a midget racing plane, capable of speeds of more than 200 miles per hour. He became the first African American to qualify for the Professional Racing Pilots Association. Later,

OPPOSITE

TOP Lewis Jackson emerged in the postwar years as a talented builder of experimental or homebuilt aircraft. He is shown here with his Jackson 10, built in 1981.

BOTTOM Jackson built the experimental J-10 aircraft with a rear mounted pusher engine in 1956. It was also a roadable type, driven hundreds of miles by Jackson.

BELOW The Lewis Jackson Concept 7 was a *roadable* airplane, with detachable wings and the option of using it as an automobile.

Loving went on to pursue a twenty-year career as an aerospace engineer at Wright-Paterson Air Force Base. In 1954, Loving flew his WR-1 aircraft from Detroit to Cuba and Jamaica, a distance of 2,200 miles. Loving's Love is now part of the aircraft collection of the Experimental Aircraft Association Museum in Oshkosh, Wisconsin.

Lewis A. Jackson joined Loving as a creative designer of experimental aircraft. His interest in aviation dated back to the Great Depression era when young blacks had few, if any, opportunities to break into the world of aeronautics. Yet, he worked tirelessly and qualified for a pilot's license, which set the stage for him to pursue a personal dream. To earn money for college, Jackson took up barnstorming in Indiana and Ohio. A talented pilot, he quickly gained the credentials to become a flight instructor with a commercial pilot's rating. He eventually caught the eye of Cornelius Coffey, who offered Jackson a position as a flight instructor at the Coffey School of Aeronautics in Chicago. With the advent of World War II, Jackson soon migrated south to the Tuskegee Army Air Field, joining the 66th Flight Training Detachment. He—and others such C. Alfred "Chief" Anderson—made a substantial contribution to the American war effort. Jackson took pride in the fact that under his guidance three groups of Tuskegee-trained pilots ranked first among the twenty-two flight schools in the Southeast Army Air Corps Training Command. While at Tuskegee, Jackson's leadership skills won him an appointment as Director of Training in Tuskegee's Division of Aeronautics, where he worked with both civilian and military trainees. In the postwar years, Jackson worked thirteen years as a flight examiner for the FAA. He also served as the president of Central State University in Ohio. Jackson managed in an impressive way to keep up his aviation pursuits while pursuing his career in higher education.

It was during the postwar years, however, that Lewis Jackson turned his attention to the challenge of designing a workable "flying car." His Jackson J-10 made its first test flight in 1956. The innovative aircraft was fitted with a 16-foot foldable wing and a pusher engine mounted at the rear of fuselage. The experimental aircraft could be driven or towed to the local airport for leisurely flights above the countryside in central Ohio. In many respects, Jackson's J-10 fit the mold of the ideal roadable aircraft—small, lightweight, portable, and easy to fly. With Neil Loving, Jackson gave witness to the latent talent within the small community of black fliers in postwar America.

RIGHT Neil Loving became a prominent black aviator in general aviation in the 1930s and 1940s.

BELOW The Loving WR-3, photographed in flight over Springfield, Ohio, in September 1976. The experimental aircraft had folding wings and could be configured to be a roadable vehicle.

BOTTOM Neil Loving's plane Loving's Love attracts a crowd of spectators.

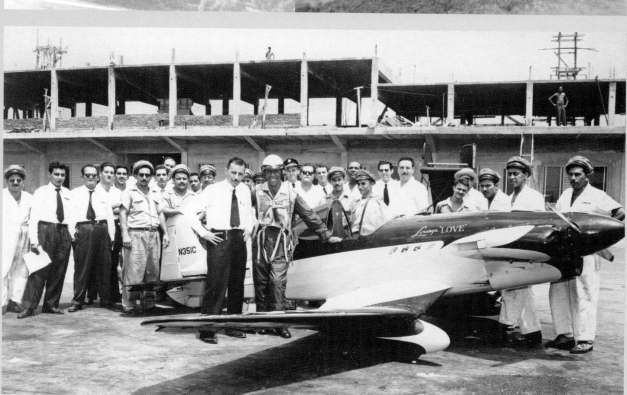

In time, the growing numbers of black pilots—some with considerable experience as military aviators—turned their eyes toward careers in commercial aviation. For years, blacks had been restricted to blue-collar service jobs as skycaps and to other forms of unskilled labor in the commercial airlines. Some black pilots had earned ratings as commercial pilots, but few, if any, cockpit assignments were open to them. Perry H. Young Jr. became one of the first black aviators to break into the elite domain of commercial aviation. He learned to fly in the late 1930s, winning the support of air enthusiasts such as Willa Brown and Cornelius Coffey. On the eve of World War II, Coffey took note of Young's skills as a pilot and hired him on as a flight instructor at the Coffey School of Aeronautics. Young eventually found his way to Tuskegee during the war, where he worked as a civilian flight instructor; after the war, racial barriers prevented him from pursuing a career in commercial aviation. Consequently, he spent ten years flying in the Caribbean as a contract pilot and mechanic, where he learned to fly helicopters—then a pioneering realm of flying. Once committed to vertical flight, Young sought an avenue to make this career path a reality. His break came in 1956 when he was hired by New York Airways to fly on a regular airline schedule of passenger, cargo, and mail flights that linked Midtown Manhattan with eight suburban airports. Young's quiet professionalism set an important precedent for a new generation of blacks seeking careers in vertical flight.

Robert "Bob" Ashby was yet another military-trained pilot seeking a career in commercial aviation. After a stint in the army reserves, Ashby transferred to the Tuskegee Army Air Field in 1944, where he earned his wings and was commissioned a second lieutenant. Although World War II ended before Ashby could fly combat, he went on to a career in the newly independent U.S. Air Force with assignments in Japan, Korea, and England. In 1965, Ashby retired from the Air Force, earning in his final year of active duty the rank of lieutenant colonel in the Strategic Air Command.

It was at this juncture in his career that Ashby decided to become a commercial airline pilot. Such a step seemed logical to him, as it was for many retiring American military pilots. Yet, Ashby realized that this step was not a routine one for a black pilot, given the fact that commercial aviation had remained segregated into the 1960s. Ashby applied for a position with United Airlines, going to Denver to serve initially as a flight operation instructor. In this role, he instructed airline pilots in classrooms, simulators, and training aircraft.

In 1954, Neil Loving flew the WR-1 from Detroit to Cuba and Jamaica.

Finding himself furloughed from United, Ashby applied to be a pilot with Frontier Airlines, where his dream of commercial airline flying became a reality: he retired as a captain in 1986 after an impressive career at the controls of the Boeing 737 and the McDonald Douglas MD-80 aircraft. His personal achievement, for the time, was unique in many respects: he remained one of a very few black commercial pilots in the decades after World War II.

What Ashby had accomplished quietly—without the klieg lights of publicity and controversy—did not become the pattern for other aspiring black pilots. Marlon Green, the most noteworthy example, discovered that his own pathway to the cockpit of a commercial airliner had been blocked. He decided to fight the racial exclusion policies in the courts—a celebrated civil rights case that went to the Supreme Court. Talented and ambitious, Green had grown up Arkansas. He joined the U.S. Air Force in 1948, on the cusp of a new era when formal segregation had ended in the military. Initially he trained as an aircraft mechanic. His first posting was at Wheeler Air Force Base in Hawaii, where he was attached to an aviation engineering squadron. While in the military, Green aspired to become a pilot, a dream that came true in 1950 when he entered flight training at historic Randolph Field in Texas. One of his fellow cadets at that time was Virgil "Gus" Grissom, who later became one of the Mercury 7 astronauts. Upon graduation, Green became an active military pilot, flying multi-engine bombers and cargo aircraft. His varied flying included the SA-16 Albatross amphibious rescue plane. He ended his Air Force career in 1957 with a flight log of more than 3,000 hours.

Just two days after his formal separation from the Air Force, Green applied for a commercial pilot slot with United Airlines. Turned away, he then sought a position at a number of other airlines, feeling that his superlative record as a military pilot would pave the way for acceptance. He applied for a pilot's position at Continental Airlines in Denver in July 1957 but was rejected. Green found a way to remain active as a pilot, accepting a job with the state of Michigan in 1957, where he remained until 1960, flying with a considerable amount of time devoted to aerial photography.

Even as he pursued this alternative, Green filed a complaint against Continental in Colorado, based on the state's anti-discrimination law. This complaint was investigated and a hearing followed. The commission determined that Continental had broken the law by rejecting Green for employment solely on the basis of race, and ordered the airline "to cease and desist" from all such discriminatory

TOP Perry Young, a pioneer in the field of vertical flight, is shown here in the cockpit of his New York Airways Vertol 44. The scheduled helicopter airline ferried passengers, cargo, and mail from Midtown Manhattan to eight suburban airports.

BOTTOM James O. Plinton Jr. (*third from right*) and his business partner Maurice DeYoung (*second from left*) gather with dignitaries in front of the Quisqueya airline's Boeing 247D in 1948. Quisqueya provided the first regular air service to the Turks and Caicos islands.

Captain David E. Harris, a pilot with American Airlines, chats with a group of young people about commercial aviation.

practices. The ruling meant that Continental had to give Green the option of enrolling in one of its training classes. This victory, however, proved to be short-lived. On review of the Commission's findings, the Colorado Supreme Court held that that the Colorado Anti-Discrimination Act of 1957—on which the Marlon Green ruling had been based—was not applicable to Continental, an interstate carrier. The state court overturned the Colorado Anti-Discrimination Commission in error, and Green found himself once again at square one.

With the able assistance of his lawyer, T. Raber Taylor, Green decided to appeal his case. On October 8, 1962, the United States Supreme Court announced that it would consider the case of the *Colorado Anti-Discrimination Commission v. Continental Air Lines, Inc.* Before the Supreme Court, under Chief Justice Earl Warren, Taylor was allowed two hours to present oral arguments, set for March 29, 1963. The case soon attracted public attention. In the end,

LEFT Marlon Green in the cockpit of the Continental Airlines Viscount

BELOW In 1965, Marlon D. Green won a long court battle with Continental Airlines over his right to fly as a commercial pilot. His case went to the Supreme Court, paving the way for significant strides in racial equality in commercial aviation.

the Supreme Court ruled unanimously in Marlon Green's favor. In two years, Green finally joined Continental as a commercial pilot, becoming a captain in 1966. He flew Continental's fast turbo-prop Vickers Viscounts out of Denver. He retired in 1978, after completing fourteen years in the cockpit. As a fitting tribute to his extraordinary career, Green was inducted into the Arkansas Aviation Historical Society Hall of Fame in 2005.

In retrospect, Marlon Green won a landmark legal case, becoming the first African American hired by a major passenger airline. He had broken the racial barrier. Change came slowly with only eighty black pilots in commercial airlines by 1976. That same year, concerned black pilots formed the Organization of Black Airline Pilots (OBAP), which, along with other groups, continues to make a concerted effort to broaden the participation of minorities in commercial aviation. For OBAP and all African American youth seeking careers in aviation, Marlon Green's lonely and determined quest for justice offered inspiration and the concrete benefit of a legal precedent establishing racial equality. The postwar years marked important strides for African Americans in both military and civil aviation.

Today modern commercial aviation includes African Americans at all levels, in the cockpit of aircraft, as members of ground crews, and increasingly as corporate leaders. Although the problem of racial discrimination persist, the days of formal discrimination are in the past.

OPPOSITE Air Force crew beside C-17 dubbed the Spirit of the Tuskegee Airmen.

RIGHT Jeanine McIntosh became the first black female aviator in the U.S. Coast Guard.

CHAPTER 7

INTO ORBIT— JOINING THE ASTRONAUT CORPS

THE 1950S GAVE RISE TO A WHOLE NEW ARENA OF human flight: rocketry and space travel. This revolution in flying was sparked by the launch of Sputnik, the world's first artificial satellite, by the Soviet Union in October 1957. Soon a space race between the United States and the Soviet Union ensued, beginning with artificial satellites, deep space probes, and finally manned space missions. Organized in 1958, the National Aeronautics and Space Administration (NASA) took charge of the American space program. In the decades that followed, NASA oversaw the Mercury, Gemini, and Apollo programs. The successful Apollo 11 Moon landing in 1969 was an important milestone. Following the Apollo missions,

Frederick D. Gregory joined the NASA space program in 1978. Gregory became the first African American to command a space shuttle flight.

NASA remained active with a variety of manned missions such as Skylab, the space shuttle flights, and joint international flights to orbiting space stations.

One of the first tasks of NASA was to recruit its first class of astronauts. The day selected for the public announcement of the astronaut program was December 17, 1958, the 55th anniversary of the historic flight of the Wright brothers at Kitty Hawk. The astronaut search had taken months to complete. Robert Gilruth and his Space Task Group took charge of the recruitment program. Initially, Gilruth's committee defined the job of astronaut in rather expansive terms, suggesting that NASA would accept physically fit applicants drawn from such widely divergent pursuits as submariners, parachute jumpers, and even explorers.

Soon, however, this open-ended approach gave way to a more demanding set of criteria: NASA decided that all future astronauts were to be drawn from the elite pool of military test pilots. In more specific terms, this meant that applicants had to be males between the ages of twenty-five and forty, no taller than five foot eleven, and have earned a college degree or equivalent experience in some appropriate technical field. Flying experience became an essential and determining factor: each astronaut had to possess a minimum of 1,500 hours—and this flight time must have included extensive cockpit time in modern jets. The initial pool consisted of some 110 candidates. This cluster of applicants was then narrowed down to sixty-nine applicants through intensive reviews, testing, and interviews. The relentless process of whittling down continued until there were seven men approved for the astronaut corps. The men who passed successfully through Gilruth's gauntlet of testing became known as the Mercury 7 astronauts. In subsequent years, additional classes of astronauts were added and the criteria expanded to include specialists outside the test pilot community.

The announcement of the nation's first class of astronauts came on April 9, 1959. As anticipated, the Mercury 7 were all military aviators, some with considerable experience as test pilots: Marine pilot John H. Glenn; navy aviators Alan B. Shepard, M. Scott Carpenter, and Walter M. Schirra; and air force fliers Virgil "Gus" Grissom, L. Gordon Cooper, and Donald K. "Deke" Slayton. The public expressed a keen interest in the new astronauts. They became famous overnight and the object of keen interest in the media. Shortly after their selection, the astronauts signed a contract with *Life* magazine for the exclusive right to record their personal stories. These men

became the human expression of the space program. Tom Wolfe, in his memorable bestseller *The Right Stuff*, captured their debut in a dramatic way: ". . . all seven, collectively, emerged in a golden haze as the seven finest pilots and bravest men in the United States. A blazing aura was upon them." America's new astronaut corps—in its first incarnation—did not include minorities or women. In a few years, as the NASA space program expanded, the astronaut corps reflected new recruitment criteria, which broadened the basis for participation. These changes mirrored new social attitudes and the evolving character of the job description for an astronaut.

Over time, African American military pilots became interested in joining NASA's astronaut corps. In 1962, Edward J. Dwight Jr. enrolled in the Aerospace Research Pilot School (ARPS) at Edwards Air Force Base in California. The high-profile program at Edwards became a training ground for future NASA astronauts. A veteran Air Force pilot with more than two thousand hours flying experience,

An Air Force pilot, Edward J. Dwight Jr. flew at Edwards Air Force as a test pilot, but he was not selected in the 1960s for the NASA astronaut program. His rejection became a matter of controversy notwithstanding the fact that NASA claimed there was no racial discrimination connected with the decision.

ABOVE Robert H. Lawrence, an Air Force major, was selected for the Manned Orbiting Laboratory (MOL). As a highly talented pilot-scientist, Lawrence was considered as a strong candidate for the NASA astronaut program. He was killed in a tragic aircraft accident in 1967.

RIGHT Robert Lawrence prior to his untimely death in a plane crash was considered by many as a candidate for the astronaut corps.

Dwight aimed to qualify as an astronaut. He had earned the rating of flight instructor and studied aeronautical engineering at Arizona State University. While at Edwards, Dwight caught the attention of President John F. Kennedy and others in Washington, who expressed great interest in an African American joining the astronaut ranks. Dwight participated with twenty-five other test pilots in the ARPS training program at Edwards. The training went through several phases, with Dwight making the cut through the first two phases of training. However, he was not selected as one of the eleven in the class to train in the ARPS six-month space-flight course. NASA later maintained that Dwight was one of a total of 136 applicants considered and was eliminated on the basis that he had not scored high enough for admittance. From NASA's viewpoint, the selection process had been open and fair, if highly demanding. The space agency pointed out that many applicants had competed for just fourteen slots in the astronaut corps. However, Dwight and his many public supporters charged NASA with racial bias. Dwight's case was debated in the years that followed. The Dwight affair took place in the same decade as the Marlon Green case, so there was widespread discussion on the need for more qualified minorities in aerospace fields.

The next black Air Force pilot to join the NASA space program was a talented pilot named Robert H. Lawrence Jr. Holding a doctorate in chemistry and an experienced military pilot with more than 2,500 hours, Lawrence participated in the Air Force's Manned Orbiting Laboratory (MOL) project. Raised in Chicago, he was thirty-two years old when he joined the MOL program. The MOL operations remained technically independent of NASA, but the pilots in the MOL training program all possessed the potential for astronaut status with NASA. All MOL trainees had completed the arduous ARPS curriculum at Edwards. On December 8, 1967, Lawrence was tragically killed when he and fellow pilot Harvey J. Royer were flying a F-104 Starfighter in a training exercise at Edwards. The men were conducting a series of high-speed landings to simulate a future landing by a spacecraft. When the F-104 touched down left of center on the runway, the landing gear collapsed and the aircraft disintegrated in a violent crash. Both men were able to eject. Royer survived, but Lawrence's parachute failed to open fully. Had he lived, Lawrence would have likely moved on to the NASA program, as did many of his colleagues when the MOL project was eventually cancelled by the Air Force.

During the early years, the NASA recruitment program opted

to select astronaut candidates from a small pool of veteran test pilots. By going to the ranks of test pilots, NASA considered only a few qualified African American as candidates. The number of black pilots in the military in the armed forces had grown dramatically in the decades following World War II, a trend fueled by the integration of the armed forces, but there were only a few who had pursued work as test pilots. Women were excluded. In time, the NASA astronaut program would add black pilots to its ranks. However, this test pilot profile soon gave way to a more varied group of candidates. The Space Shuttle program, by definition, called for crews with diverse and complementary specializations—there were now mission specialists, not just pilots. Accordingly, the astronaut corps included scientists, physicians, and engineers. Astronauts were responsible for a wide range of scientific experiments and non-piloting roles on the Space Shuttle. Advanced degrees in science and technical fields became essential for the Space Shuttle program to function properly. The astronaut corps changed dramatically. At the end of the twentieth century, minorities and women would play diverse roles as pilots, mission specialists, and scientists in America's space program.

The first African American to participate fully as a member of the NASA astronaut corps was Guion "Guy" Bluford. He grew up in Philadelphia where his father was a mechanical engineer, his mother a school teacher. Bluford demonstrated an early interest in aeronautics, building model aircraft and dreaming of a career in aviation. During his high school years his interests included reading, chess, and stamp collecting. Once admitted to Penn State University, Bluford pursued his passion for aeronautics, graduating in 1964 with a degree in aeronautical engineering. He then joined the U.S. Air Force, where he successfully earned his wings as a fighter pilot.

Bluford's training as a fighter pilot coincided with the deepening U.S. involvement in the Vietnam War. He attended pilot training at Williams Air Force Base in Arizona. He went to F-4C crew training in Arizona and Florida and was deployed to Vietnam, attached to 557th Tactical Fighter Squadron at Cam Ranh Bay. His tour of duty in Vietnam involved a total of 144 air combat missions, including ten over North Vietnam. While on active duty, he earned numerous medals, including the Air Force Commendation medal. Following his service in Vietnam, Bluford was posted at Sheppard Air Force Base in Texas, where he served as a flight instructor. Later, among several postings, he remained active with flight training, accumulating a total of 4,600 hours in a variety of jet aircraft. In 1968, he earned his

Guion "Guy" Bluford became the first African American to fly in the Space Shuttle program. He came to NASA from the Air Force where he had flown in the Vietnam War.

Guy Bluford and Sally Ride reflected the changing character of the astronaut program. With the Space Shuttle program there were increased opportunities for talented African Americans and women to participate in the space program.

doctorate in aerospace engineering and laser physics at the Air Force Institute of Technology.

Given his stellar career and academic credentials, Bluford joined the NASA space program in 1978. Five years later, he flew his first shuttle mission (STS-8 on August 30, 1983), becoming the first African American to travel into space. On this inaugural flight, Bluford orbited Earth ninety-eight times. He served as a mission specialist on four shuttle flights, logging 688 hours in space. Bluford remained active as an astronaut until his retirement in 1993. While in the shuttle program, he worked in a variety of technical tasks, including the Space Station Freedom operations, the Remote Manipulator System, the Skylab systems and experiments.

In 1978, Frederick D. Gregory joined the NASA space program, a part of the same class as Bluford. Gregory, a former Air Force officer and veteran of the Vietnam War, grew up in Washington, D.C. In 1964, he graduated from the Air Force Academy. His military service included training in helicopters at Stead Air Force Base in Nevada, and his first military assignment was at Van Air Force Base in Oklahoma in October 1965. Assigned to a forward air unit in Vietnam, Gregory flew hazardous duty as an H-43 combat rescue pilot at Danang, accumulating 550 combat missions. Once he completed his tour of duty in Vietnam, he flew fixed-wing aircraft, training at Randolph Air Force Base and was attached to a F-4 unit at Davis-Monthan air base in Arizona. Given his aptitude for flying, Gregory attended the Naval Test Pilot School, graduating in June 1971. By the 1970s, Gregory joined the 4950th Test Wing at historic Wright-Paterson Air Force Base in Ohio, where he was assigned to test flying duties with both helicopter and fixed-wing aircraft. Later he was detailed to the NASA Langley Research Center in Virginia.

While flying at Langley, NASA selected Gregory for the astronaut corps. At this juncture in his career, he had logged nearly seven thousand hours flying in some fifty different types of aircraft. NASA recognized Gregory's superlative skills and eventually assigned him to a series of demanding tasks in the Space Shuttle program. Initially, he was involved in technical assignments: working with checkout and launch support for the early flights of the Orbiter (STS-1 and STS-2), communications (CAPCOM), and programs for safety and training. In 1985, Gregory served as pilot on the Orbiter *Challenger* on a mission (STS-51B) that included a series of scientific experiments and the deployment of the Northern Utah Satellite (NUSAT). His next major assignment came with the night launch of STS-33 in November 1989. On this mission, Gregory established a noteworthy milestone—the first African American to serve as commander of a space shuttle flight. On the Orbiter *Discovery*, Gregory and his crew carried into orbit a primary Department of Defense payloads. It was a five-day mission that recorded some seventy-nine orbits of Earth. Gregory would command another space shuttle mission in 1991 (STS-44), which completed 110 orbits. A few years later, Gregory accepted a position at NASA Headquarters, where he held a number of senior administrative positions, serving for a brief time as the acting NASA administrator. He also served as associate administrator in the Office of Safety and Mission Assurance (1992–2001), associate administrator for the Office of Space Flight (2001–2002), and NASA deputy administrator (2002–2005). Fred Gregory retired in October 2005, having completed more than a quarter century of service at NASA.

The contributions of astronauts Bluford and Gregory to the NASA space program were substantial, setting the stage for other

TOP LEFT Charles Bolden stands next to his aircraft trainer.

TOP RIGHT Charles F. Bolden graduated from the U.S. Naval Academy in 1968. Bolden served as a pilot with the Naval Test Center before joining NASA as an astronaut.

LEFT Mae C. Jamison became an important African American astronaut with eclectic interests in science, photography, languages, and dance. She flew as a mission specialist on the space shuttle Endeavour in 1992, completing 127 orbits of Earth.

black astronauts—men and women—to follow them. Charles Bolden also was a part of the early contingent of black astronauts, serving as a pilot on the Orbiter *Columbia* (STS-61C in 1986) and the *Discovery* (STS-31 in 1990) and, finally, as the mission commander on the Orbiter *Atlantis* (STS-45 in 1992). In time, the participation of black astronauts ceased to be a novelty. There was increasingly less need to mark each flight of an African American as another first for NASA. This altered environment signaled the strides made by NASA in the 1980s and 1990s to integrate fully its space flight operations.

Pioneering black astronaut Ronald E. McNair gave his life in one of the most tragic episodes in the history of the space age: the *Challenger* disaster of January 26, 1986. Born in South Carolina, McNair displayed an impressive aptitude for science as a youth. In 1971, he obtained his undergraduate physics degree (magna cum laude) from North Carolina A & T State University. Graduate work then followed at the Massachusetts Institute of Technology, where he obtained a doctorate in physics. While pursuing his doctorate at MIT, McNair

Ronald McNair became a mission specialist in the Space Shuttle program in the 1980s. He held a doctorate in physics from the Massachusetts Institute of Technology.

performed some of the early work in laser physics. His scholarly work won wide praise, allowing him to present research papers at home and in Europe. His personal interests included the martial arts and the saxophone. Hughes Research Laboratories in California hired McNair as a staff physicist, where he continued his work in the field of lasers. In 1978, NASA selected McNair as an astronaut candidate, joining the same class with Bluford and Gregory.

McNair completed his intensive training at NASA in August 1979, which then qualified him for a future space shuttle mission. His first opportunity to reach earth orbit came in 1984, when he was selected as a mission specialist on the *Challenger* (STS-41B). This particular flight involved the deployment of two communications satellites. McNair played a pivotal role in this maneuver as the first astronaut to operate the arm to position EVA crewmen around the payload bay of the shuttle. McNair's excellent work on this mission won him praise. At this juncture in his career, he had logged more than 190 hours in Earth orbit.

NASA selected McNair to fly again on January 28, 1986 on the *Challenger*, a space shuttle that had completed nine successful missions. The fateful flight of the *Challenger* on this mission (STS-51-L) would result in the death of the entire crew. McNair's fellow crewmembers were Dick Scobee, commander; Michael J. Smith, pilot; Ellison D. Onizuka and Judith Resnik, mission specialists; and G. B. Jarvis and Christa McAuliffe, payload specialists. Millions of viewers watched *Challenger*'s launch on television. There was keen interest in the flight because McAuliffe, a school teacher and mother of two, had been selected from a competition of ten thousand entries to participate in a program called the Teacher in Space Program (TISP). Many schools watched the televised launch because of her participation on the mission. Given the wide interest generated in the launch, President Ronald Reagan delayed his State of the Union address to accommodate the historic flight from Cape Kennedy. The launch had been postponed six times as a result of poor weather and technical problems. At the time of the launch, outside temperature was 36 degrees Fahrenheit (2 degrees Celsius), a very cold day along the Florida coast.

The *Challenger* accident came just seventy-three seconds into the flight, even as the shuttle remained visible on its ascent into the upper atmosphere. The shuttle did not explode, but fell apart at an altitude of some 46,000 feet. Film later showed the telltale flicker of flames, followed by a well-defined flame along the surface of the huge external fuel tank. The breakup caused a massive spill of liquid oxygen and hydrogen, which suddenly created a huge fireball. *Challenger* was torn apart, scattering various rocket components over a wide area.

On February 3, President Reagan organized a commission to examine the causes of the accident, an investigative group headed by former attorney general William P. Rogers. When the report was released in June of that year, the cause of the accident was traced to a failure of the O-ring seals that prevented the leak of hot gases from the solid rocket booster. The extremely cold temperatures had contributed to the failure of the seal.

At the memorial service in Houston for the astronauts, President

ABOVE Bernard Harris, a veteran of NASA's Space Shuttle program, represents a second generation of African Americans in space, following in the footsteps of Bluford, Gregory, and Bolden.

RIGHT Robert L. Curbeam, a graduate of the U.S. Naval Academy, joined the NASA space program in 1994. Curbeam logged some 901 hours in space, including seven EVA's or "space walks."

Reagan urged Americans to remember the *Challenger* Seven, whose lives had been filled with "dedication, honor, and an unquenchable desire to explore this mysterious and beautiful universe." He then memorialized each astronaut. When he came to the sole African American crewmember, President Reagan stated: "We remember Ronald McNair, who said that he learned perseverance in the cotton fields of South Carolina. His dream was to live aboard a space station, performing experiments and playing his saxophone in the weightlessness of space; Ron, we will miss your saxophone and we will build your space station." (*Houston Chronicle*). NASA did not launch another shuttle into space until September 1988 with the launch of the Orbiter *Discovery*.

In the years that followed, a number of black astronauts participated in the ongoing NASA space shuttle program. For example, Robert L. Curbeam Jr., a graduate of the U.S. Naval Academy and former naval aviator, carved out an impressive career in the space program. As a latter-day entrant, he joined in 1994. As an active NASA astronaut, Curbeam logged 901 hours in space, including 7 space walks. He flew on the space shuttles *Discovery* (1997 and 2006) and *Atlantis* (2001). Other experienced black astronauts include Bernard A. Harris Jr., Leland D. Melvin, and Winston E. Scott. These men—and others—followed in the tradition of Bluford, Gregory, and Bolden.

As NASA evolved, the number of women astronauts expanded. Soon African American women found their place in the ever-changing astronaut corps. Mae C. Jemison became an early pioneer. A native of Alabama, Jemison grew up in Chicago and, as a student at Stanford, demonstrated eclectic interests in science, photography, languages (Russian, Swahili, and Japanese), and dance. In 1981, she earned a doctorate in medicine from Cornell University. After completing an internship in Los Angeles, she served as a medical officer for the Peace Corps in Sierra Leone and Liberia in West Africa. In 1987, Jemison began training for the NASA astronaut corps. After a series of technical assignments at the Kennedy Space Center, she flew as a mission specialist on the flight of the space shuttle *Endeavour* (STS-47 Spacelab-J) in 1992. On this eight-day mission, she recorded a total of 127 orbits of the Earth. As a mission specialist, she worked as a coinvestigator on a bone cell research experiment. Jemison left NASA in 1993, but other African American women have since followed in her footsteps: Stephanie Wilson, Yvonne Cagle, and Joan Higginbotham.

TOP Isaac Gillam IV (*left*), a Special Assistant for Space Transportation Systems at NASA, served as the director of the Dryden Research Center at Edwards Air Force Base in California.

BOTTOM Vance Marchbanks, an African American flight surgeon, served with the mission control team in Kano, Nigeria, for the historic John Glenn orbital mission in February 1962. Marchbanks had served in World War II with the Tuskegee airmen in Italy.

The active participation of African Americans in the NASA space program has extended to the nonflying dimensions of the space program. Colonel Vance Marchbanks, a Tuskegee airman and World War II veteran, played a significant role in the early NASA Mercury flights. Marchbanks, a medical doctor, monitored the vital physiological signs of John Glenn on his historic orbital flight in February 1962. Aerospace engineer Dr. Robert Shurney assisted with the design of technology for use in zero gravity, most notably designing utensils for food consumption and lightweight aluminum tires for the lunar rover used on the 1972 Apollo 16 lunar mission. William Conway and George Carruthers also made substantial contributions to the space program with their design of an ultraviolet camera for the NASA lunar missions. Scores of other African Americans have filled key staff and research positions at NASA since the 1960s.

Michael P. Anderson graduated from the University of Washington in 1981 and went on to earn a doctorate in physics from Creighton University a decade later. He was an Air Force veteran who served as an EC 135 pilot, flying as both a command pilot and flight instructor with the 920th Air Refueling Squadron in Michigan between 1991 and 1992. He later became an instructor pilot with the 380th Air Refueling Wing in New York between 1992 and 1995.

Anderson joined NASA in March 1995. His first space shuttle mission was on the *Endeavour* (STS-89 in 1998)—the eighteenth space shuttle rendezvous with the Russian Mir space station. The *Endeavour* docked with Mir to transfer an American astronaut and supplies, including scientific instruments. The flight took more than 8 days, covered some 3.6 million miles, and included 138 orbits of Earth. For Anderson, the space mission was an exhilarating experience, a milestone in his burgeoning career as an astronaut.

His second space shuttle mission was a sixteen-day flight on the *Columbia*, from January to February 2003, during which they would conduct a series of scientific experiments. As the Orbiter *Columbia* reentered the atmosphere on the morning of February 1 and made its descent over eastern California, it experienced a rapid increase in temperature in the left wheel well. As it moved across New Mexico, the situation worsened, leading to the catastrophic disintegration of the spacecraft, killing all on board: Michael Anderson and his fellow crewmembers Rick D. Husband, commander; William C. McCool, pilot; and Kalpana Chawla, David M. Brown, Laurel B. Clark, and Ilan Ramon, mission specialists.

The orbiter had sustained wing damage at the launch because of a chunk of insulation from a fuel tank. Michael Anderson is remembered for his extraordinary talent and dedication as a mission specialist. He joined Ronald McNair as the second African American to die in the American space program. The NASA missions were a mix of triumph and tragedy. Anderson received a posthumous Congressional Space Medal of Honor, plus other medals and awards for his exemplary service to his country and the cause of space exploration.

Charles Bolden—a one-time crewmember on the *Columbia*—spoke for all astronauts when he described the unique experience of riding atop a rocket into outer space and seeing the continent of Africa: "It is absolutely breathtaking . . . I was just flabbergasted from the very beginning to find that it is just so massive, even from three hundred miles out in space, that there's just no way in the world that you can comprehend it all in a short span of, say, five or six days."

The first appearance of African American astronauts—as both command pilots and mission specialists—marked a significant benchmark in the world of aerospace, which started when Guy Bluford qualified for the astronaut corps in 1978. By the 1980s, minorities and women were routinely assigned as crew for Space Shuttle missions. For the first time, the expanded ranks of astronauts mirrored more accurately the diverse character of American society. Ironically, in the 1980s and 1990s, NASA faced increased difficulties in the recruitment of minorities. Some of the most talented pilots, scientists, and engineers were drawn to more lucrative careers in the civilian sector. African Americans will certainly continue to play a vital role in America's evolving space program.

Over the decades, since the Wright brothers first flew in 1903, there have been important strides toward racial equality, always as a result of struggle and persistence. Flight—as with other arenas of modern life—cannot be separated from its social and cultural moorings. Race persists as a key factor. Consequently, the story of African American pilots and astronauts remains a compelling theme in the American experience.

SOURCES AND FURTHER READING

In recent years, the historical literature dealing with the role of African Americans in aerospace history has expanded dramatically. Interested readers may find a diverse array of new biographies, histories, and special studies, some of which are specifically targeted to children and young adults. At the core of this bibliography are a number of excellent scholarly studies based on primary sources and dealing with broad interpretative themes related to race and the American experience. No less important is the growing list of books designed for the general audience, which often are more celebratory in approach and offering many fascinating details, anecdotes, and firsthand accounts. Even more numerous have been the steady stream of articles in magazines and historical journals, too numerous, in fact, to list here. Films and television documentaries have supplemented this body of historical literature. Online resources have provided researchers with instantaneous access to a vast realm of historical data and literature—always reflecting diverging standards of accuracy.

There are several excellent sources for authoritative background material on black aerospace pioneers, which shaped the narrative for *Black Wings: Courageous Stories of African Americans in Aviation and Space History.* Doris Rich's *Queen Bess: Daredevil Aviator,* Washington, D.C.: Smithsonian Institution Press, 1993, remains the definitive biography of Bessie Coleman. There is also the older first-hand account by William J. Powell Jr. in his quasi-autobiographical *Black Wings,* published in 1934, and later reprinted with an introduction by Von Hardesty, in *Black Aviator: The Story of William J. Powell,* Washington, D.C.: Smithsonian Institution, 1994. Philip S. Hart's brief, though insightful, *Flying Free: America's First Black Aviators,* Minneapolis, Minnesota: Lerner Publications, 1996, offers yet another perspective on the early years. Anyone researching on the Tuskegee airmen will benefit from two key sources: Stanley Sandler, *Segregated Skies, All Black Combat Squadrons in WW II,*

Washington, D.C.: Smithsonian Institution Press, 1992, and the memoir of Benjamin O. Davis Jr., which covers in detail the World War II years, *Benjamin O. Davis, Jr., American: An Autobiography*, Washington, D.C.: Smithsonian Institution, 1991. One classic study of the integration of the armed forces remains Alan L. Gropman's excellent *The Air Force Integrates, 1945–1964*, Washington, D.C., second edition, 1998. For general reference and biographical materials, the reader is directed to Betty Gubert, Miriam Sawyer, and Caroline M. Fannin, *Distinguished African Americans in Aviation and Space Science*, New York: Oryx Press, 2001.

Listed below are selected titles now available for further reading on the role of African Americans in aerospace history.

Astor, Gerald. *The Right to Fight: A History of African Americans in the Military*, Novato, California: Presidio Press, 1998.

Astor, G. *The Right to Fight: A History of African Americans in the Military*. California: Presidio Press, 1998.

Bragg, Janet. *Soaring Above Setbacks: The Autobiography of Janet Harmon Bragg, African American Aviator, as told to Marjorie M. Kriz*. Washington, D.C.: Smithsonian Institution Press, 1996.

Broadnax, Samuel L. *Blue Skies, Black Wings: African American Pioneers of Aviation*, New York: Praeger, 2007.

Bucholtz, Chris and Jim Laurier. *332ⁿᵈ Fighter Group—Tuskegee Airmen*, London: Osprey Publishing, 2007.

Cooper, M. *The Double V Campaign: African Americans in WW II*. New York: Lodestar Books, Penguin Putnam, Inc., 1998.

Craven, Wesley Frank and James Lea Cate, editors, *The Army Air Forces in World War II*, volumes II and VI, Chicago: University of Chicago Press, 1949, 1955.

Dalfume, Richard M. *Desegregation of the U. S. Armed Forces: Flying on Two Fronts, 1939–1953*, Columbia: University of Missouri Press, 1969.

Dryden, Charles W. *A-Train: Memoirs of a Tuskegee Airmen*. Tuscaloosa, Alabama: University of Alabama Press, 1997.

Francis, Charles. *Tuskegee Airmen: The Men Who Changed a Nation*, Boston: Bruce Humphries, 1955, 1988.

Freyberg, Elizabeth A. H. *Bessie Coleman: The Brownskin Lady Bird*. New York: Garland Publishing, 1994.

Hart Philip S. and Martha Cosgrove, _Bessie Coleman_, Minneapolis, Minnesota: Lerner Publications, 2005.

Holway, John B. _Red Tails, Black Wings: The Men of America's Black Air Force_, Las Cruces, New Mexico: Yucca Tree, 1997.

Homar, Lynn and Thomas Reilly. _Black Knights: The Story of the Tuskegee Airmen_, Greta, Louisiana: Pelican Publishing Company, 2001.

Jakeman, R. _The Divided Skies: Establishing Segregated Flight Training at Tuskegee_ 1934–1942, Tuscaloosa, Alabama: University of Alabama Press, 1992.

Lee, Ulysses. _The Employment of Negro Troops_, Washington, D.C.: U.S. Army Center of Military History, 1966; reprint 1986, 1990.

Lindbergh, R. _Nobody Owns the Sky: The Story of Bessie Coleman_. Massachusetts, Candlewick Press, 1998.

Loving, Neil. _Loving's Love_, Washington, D.C.: Smithsonian Institution Press, 1994.

McGee Smith, Charlene E. _Tuskegee Airman: The Biography of Charles F. McGee, Air Force Fighter Combat Record Holder_, Boston: Branden Publishing Company, 1999.

McKissack, P. and F. McKissack. _Red-Tail Angels: The Story of the Tuskegee Airmen_. New York: Walker & Company, 1995.

Osur, Alan, _Blacks in the Army Air Forces in World War II_, Washington, D.C., 1977.

Patterson, Elois. _Memoirs of the Late Bessie Coleman, Aviatrix_. Published privately by Elois Patterson in 1969.

Perret, Geoffrey. _Winged Victory: The Army Air Forces in World War II_, New York: Random House, 1998.

Pisano, Dominick. _To Fill the Skies_, Washington, D.C.: Smithsonian Institution Press, 1993 and 2001.

Scott, Lawrence P. and William M. Womack Sr., _Double V: The Civil Rights Struggle of the Tuskegee Airmen_, East Lansing, Michigan: Michigan State University Press, 1994.

Warren, James C. _The Freeman Field Mutiny_, Vacaville, California: Conyers Publishing Company, 1996.

ONLINE RESOURCES

http://www.nasm.si.edu

The National Air and Space Museum's website, Black Wings, African American Pioneer Aviators, offers the teacher guide

African American Pioneers in Aviation: 1920–Present as well as free teacher resource materials, online activities for students, and information about school tours.

http://www.obap.org
   Organization of Black Airline Pilots (OBAP)
   Information about OBAP's goals and programs

http://www.aero-space.nasa.gov/edu/links.htm
   NASA Online Resources for Educators

http://www.tuskegeeairmen.org
   The Tuskegee Airmen International site offers a history of the Tuskegee experience and photographs of the planes the airmen flew. It also lists local chapters of the organization.

http://www.cr.nps.gov/museum/exhibits/tuskegee
   The National Park Service site provides historical information on individual Tuskegee Airmen, an overview of the program, and information on this new Park Service site at Tuskegee Institute that will commemorate the airmen's experience.

http://raahistory.com
   The Real African American Heroes site offers information on astronauts and other aviators.

http://www.afroam.org/history/tusk/tuskmain.html
   The AFRO-America's Black History Museum site has a section entitled "The Tuskegee Airmen: The Sky Was the Limit," which includes information on African American war correspondents in World War II and on Tuskegee and other African Americans.

http://www.pbs.org/blackpress/news_bios/courier.html
   Visit the PBS website "The Black Press: Soldiers Without Swords" to explore the history of four newspapers and to learn about the men and women who helped shape the history of the black press. This site also contains Double V information.

PHOTOGRAPHY CREDITS

ABBREVIATIONS: T = TOP; B = BOTTOM; L = LEFT; R = RIGHT; C = CENTER

Black Wings Exhibit and Book Collection, National Air and Space Museum Acc. No. 1992-0060: 9 (SI 99-15416), 11tl (SI 99-15415), 18 (SI 99-15417), 27 (SI 99-15419), 30t (SI 99-15418), 49 (SI 99-15420), 79tl (SI 91-6604), 79tr (SI 91-6599), 115 (SI 99-15263). Library of Congress, Prints and Photographics Division, Toni Frissell Collection: 91br (LC-DIG-ppmsca-13259), 96bl (LC-DIG-ppmsca-13263), 96tl (LC-DIG-ppmsca-13269), 96bl (LC-DIG-ppmsca-11759), 99 (LC-DIG-ppmsca-13248), 100 (LC-DIG-ppmsca-13245), 117b (LC-DIG-ppmsca-13264). Manuscripts, Archives and Special Collections, Washington State University Libraries, Pangborn Collection: 13 (B6F216GatesCircusAd). National Aeronautics and Space Administration: 152 (GPN-2004-00020), 159, 160, 162tr, 165t (GPN-2006-000022), 165b (JSC2001-00079). National Aeronautics and Space Administration, via National Air and Space Museum, Smithsonian Institution: 162tl (SI 98-15713). National Air and Space Museum, Smithsonian Institution: 5 (SI 88-7983), 7 (SI 91-6283), 34 (SI 99-15423), 35 (SI 99-15422), 36 (SI 15486), 37 (SI 82-14246), 40b (SI 91-15487), 42 (SI 83-99), 47 (SI 83-97), 53t (SI 90-6807), 53b (SI 90-6808), 54 (SI 90-6809), 56t (90-6811), 56b (SI 90-6810), 58 (SI 90-6812), 60 (SI 99-15504), 63 (SI 94-3550), 64t (SI 99-15429), 64b (SI 99-15430), 67 (SI 99-15431), (SI 99-15432), 68 (SI 90-7010), 71 (SI 99-15428), 72r (SI 99-15440), 73t (SI 91-14671), 75 (SI 99-15437), 76t Top (SI 99-15433), 76b (SI 99-15441), 78 (SI 99-15442), 79b (SI 99-15434/SI 99-15435), 81 (SI 99-15436), 82t (SI 99-15443), 82br (SI 99-15444), 83t (SI 99-15508), 83b (SI 99-15511), 87tr (SI 86-11270), 88 (SI 99-15449), 90 (SI 99-15452), 91t (SI 86-11269), 91cl (SI 94-35490), 91cr (SI 99-15451), 92tr (SI 99-15463), 92cr (SI 99-15447), 93t (SI 99-15465), 94t (SI 99-15460), 94b (SI 99-15522), 95 (SI 99-15469), 98 (SI 99-15520), 101bl (SI 99-15466), 105b (SI 82-11917), 111b (SI 99-15513), 112t (SI 98-15731), 112b (SI 99-15458), 113t (SI 99-15457), 116 (SI 99-15454), 117t (SI 99-15455), 118cl (SI 99-15516), 123 (SI 99-15508), 124t (SI 91-6588), 124b (SI 99-15481), 127t (SI 99-15523), 127bl (SI 99-15524), 127br (SI 99-15480), 128b (SI 94-3559), 131 (SI 99-15485), 132 (SI 99-15491), 133t (SI 92-4076), 133b (SI 91-6284), 134l (SI 99-15484), 134tr (SI 99-15490), 134br (SI 90-1032), 135 (SI 91-6591), 136t (SI 93-16145), 136b (SI 99-15487), 137 (SI 99-15488), 138 (SI 99-15492),139t (SI 99-15493), 139b (SI 99-15494), 140t (SI 82-14293), 140b (SI 82-14289), 141 (SI 82-14288), 143tl (SI 99-15527), 143tr (SI 99-15495), 143b (SI 99-15527), 145 (SI 99-15495), 146t (SI 99-15496), 146b (99-15497), 148 (SI 99-15499), 155 (SI 13258), 156t (SI 99-15501), 163 (SI 99-15502), 166t (99-15500), 166b (94-7505). National Air and Space Museum, Smithsonian Institution— B. O. Davis Collection: 118tl, 118tr, 118bl, 118br, 118cl. National Archives and Records Administration: 73b (208-FS-872-3), 74 (208-MO-120H-29054), 80 (208-NP-2W-2), 87tl (111-SC-184968), 92br (80-G-54413), 93b (208-AA-49E-1-1), 103 (208-AA-102E-5), 110 (208-MO-18K-32983), 113b (208-AA-47E-1). United States Air Force: 150. United States Air Force, via National Air and Space Museum, Smithsonian Institution: 70 (SI 97-17235), 101cl (SI 99-15461), 105t (SI 97-17232), 106 (SI 99-15470), 109 (SI 99-15459), 111t (SI 99-15453), 114t (SI 99-15478), 114b (SI 99-15445), 129 (SI 99-15482). United States Coast Guard: 151. United States Navy, Naval Historical Center: 120. Courtesy of Greenwich Workshop: 107. Courtesy of the Paul Roales Collection: 53c. Courtesy of Paula Green: 149t, 149b. Courtesy of Ted Hamady: 17, 84. Courtesy of The Wolf Aviation Fund: 4. Farwell T. Brown Photographic Archive, Ames Public Library, Ames, Iowa: 46. Courtesy of Von Hardesty: ii, 6, 11br, 12, 14, 20, 22, 24, 25, 28, 29, 30bl, 30br, 32l, 38, 40t, 66, 72t, 82bl, 87b, 89, 92l, 96r, 97t, 97b, 101tl, 101r, 102, 104t, 104b, 108t, 108b, 111c, 126, 128t, 156b.

INDEX